From the Pinnacle of the Temple

Charles Farah, Jr., Ph.D.

Logos International
Plainfield, New Jersey

Dedication

To encourage those for whom "a
faith formula" has not worked and to
liberate those who have come under
unjust condemnation or, worse yet,
lost their faith completely.

Scripture references are from the Revised Standard Version unless noted as
KJV (King James Version), TLB (The Living Bible), NAS (New American
Standard), NEB (New English Bible), TAB (The Amplified Bible), NIV (New
International Version) or Phillips (J.B. Phillips translation).

Contents

Foreword

This book began a number of years ago when I met with Chuck and Jo Ann Farah in Tulsa, Oklahoma. Deeply concerned about the excesses stemming from the extremist "faith teachers," Dr. Farah had written an excellent paper on "Faith vs. Presumption" which had been published by the Presbyterian Charismatic Communion. I visited with the Farahs for several days—while ministering at Tulsa Christian Fellowship—encouraging him to enlarge his thoughts into a book.

There are so many excesses in the Christian world in the area of faith. They range all the way from no faith at all to the handling of snakes. By far the most serious extreme centers around the "confess it and it's yours" teaching—without counting the cost, meeting the conditions, or taking into account the larger purpose of the sovereignty of God. Chuck Farah was the only man I knew who had the scholarship, the insight and personal experience necessary to write a book on balance. The fact he lived in Tulsa, the home of the strongest teaching on the subject, qualified him even more.

A year later Chuck was with me on a camping expedition in the Sinai Wilderness. One evening near Rephidim, close to the spot where Moses held up his arms—supported by Aaron and Hur—while Joshua defeated the Amalakites in the valley below, the two of us left the group. Alone in the twilight, we climbed to the top of a huge boulder overlooking the wadi. It was almost night and the awesome silence of the Sinai descended upon us. We stretched out on our backs on top of the rock—still warm from the blazing sun which by now had disappeared toward Egypt. The towering, craggy mountains surrounded us. Overhead the dark sky was beginning to twinkle with brilliance.

We prayed aloud. During the prayer time Chuck prayed for this book—praying that when it finally materialized it would bless, and not divide, the kingdom. I prayed that God would give my friend a special gift of writing obstetrics, to birth on paper that which the Holy Spirit had conceived in his heart.

The gestation period for each book is different—but the travail and labor of delivery is always intense. When it came time to write, Chuck was unsure. We talked many times. I finally agreed to help him with his writing. At one point he even asked me to write the book for him. Later we revised that to ''by'' Dr. Charles Farah, Jr., ''with'' Jamie Buckingham. No delivery of a first draft was ever more difficult, for he was working without the benefit of a literary midwife. I'm not surprised, for I knew the book was destined to bless the kingdom.

But when Chuck sent his completed chapters for me to rewrite, edit, and add my own material, there was almost nothing for me to do. My Sinai prayer—and his—had been answered. So lucid was his writing, so complete his content, so insightful his direction that all I did was make minor corrections—and urge him to add the chapter about the homegoing of our dear, mutual friend, Martha Sanders.

It is his book, as God has given him wisdom.

I firmly believe this book will find its place as one of the most relevant and balanced books of our generation. Few, if any, more important publications will appear this year.

Jamie Buckingham
Melbourne, Florida

1

Learning from Disaster

My confusion surrounding healing, and the place of faith in the healing process, was intensified when I learned of the Larry Parker tragedy.

Wesley, the Parkers' diabetic son, was twelve years old when the Parkers took the long, hard step they felt their faith required. They asked the church to pray for Wesley. Faith, they believed, meant withdrawing all medication. They thought they had to go one way or the other, but not both. They stopped the insulin. Three days later Wesley was dead.

I could not escape the hollow feeling in the pit of my stomach as I read the news story of Wesley's death. The parents had been arrested and charged with manslaughter and criminal neglect. All because they wanted to believe God.

I visualized them sitting beside Wesley's bed, watching him slip into a coma, praying, beseeching God, praising

Him for the healing, giving positive confession, knowing the insulin would restore him to life, yet wanting to trust entirely in God. It was the same process I had been through. Only in their case it involved more than an itchy scalp—it involved the life of their son.

I could feel their spiritual anguish as they cried out to God: "We're standing on your Word. You said it and we believe it. 'But he was wounded for our transgressions, he was bruised for our iniquities; upon him was the chastisement that made us whole, and with his stripes we are healed' (Isa. 53:5). We believe your Word, Lord. We believe our son is already healed."

Even after Wesley died, the parents' faith did not falter. They remained firm and steadfast, fully expecting a Lazarus-type resurrection. They believed for "the greater miracle"—that God would raise Wesley from the dead. They had faith to move mountains—but nothing happened. "We knew in our minds," Larry said, "that Jesus never fails. Yet our son was dead." Harsh reality burst over resurrection hope, drowning it in a sea of guilt and remorse. For three years Larry staggered in a dark night of the soul, clinging desperately to his faith in Jesus. He learned the Psalmist's truth, "If I make my bed in Sheol, thou art there" (Ps. 139:8). Psalm 23 taught him that "walking through the valley of shadow of death" he need "fear no evil."

The criminal trial followed—parents accused of the death of the son they loved more than life itself.

Larry would never forget the shame and humiliation of that trial, the indignant looks of neighbors who became cool, and the turning away of good Christian friends who could never forgive him for his tragic mistake.

Despite the fact that Larry never refuted the doctrine which led him into error, he did experience the grace of God in a dimension he'd never known before. Reflecting on the episode, he wrote: "In the following months the Lord dealt with us in a most loving, kind and gentle way. His reproof was filled with compassion and He revealed to us one step at a time our tragic error."

During this whole agonizing experience, his wife too experienced the grace of God in a new way. Christ carried her through on the wings of the "peace that passeth understanding," except for one agonizing time when she asked why she couldn't express the grief she knew she had. For the moment God lifted His supernatural peace and she was overcome by tears that could not flow fast enough and by pain so excruciating she could not endure it. She was driven to the brink of insanity as her torture became a physical pressure that nearly burst within her. She cried out, "Oh, God! I can't stand it! Please remove it, I cannot live with this pain."

Miraculously, God lifted the excruciating pain and she was once again enveloped by the One who bore her griefs and "carried her sorrows." Larry, on the other hand, continued to feel the conflict between love and faith in his own heart. His love had wanted to give Wesley the insulin he knew would save his life, but his faith had prohibited the giving of the life-giving drug. What a struggle: faith versus love! His "faith" led him to erroneously believe: "Give in to insulin and it will cost him his healing. Use medicine and the cure will vanish." Love said, "Give it to him anyhow, he's dying. Love is greater than faith." Tragically, the wrong kind of "faith" won out. Reflecting on this, Larry observed, "To withhold medicine, especially life-giving medicine, is a very presumptuous act on our part."

As I struggled through the Parker incident I saw myself. And I heard the teachings of others. But in it all I discovered a new glimpse of a truth which had previously eluded me. There is a difference between faith and presumption. Was it possible that a lot of what passes for "faith" is really presumption? Larry Parker, convicted of slaughtering his own son, wisely concluded, "Until God reveals the healing, He expects us to do everything on our part to ease pain and suffering."

In its primary meaning, presumption is "the act of presuming, specifically an overstepping of proper bounds, forwardness, effrontery." What happens when Christians "overstep the proper bounds"? Does God miraculously interpose himself between their foolishness and the tragic consequences of their mistaken actions? Is there such a thing as the sin of presumption? Does the Bible have anything to say about it?

Shortly after reading Larry Parker's story, I began to search the Bible concerning this difference between faith and presumption. I discovered no less than eleven references in the Bible referring to presumption. All but one are in the Old Testament. The one exception is 2 Peter 2:10. In every case, presumption is a deadly sin. In fact, I was astonished to discover that in nine verses in the Old Testament the direct consequences of presumption were death. In other words, presumption is just as deadly a sin as witchcraft. Numbers 15:30-31 states, "But the soul that doeth ought presumptuously, whether he be born in the land, or a stranger, the same reproacheth the Lord; and that soul shall be utterly cut off. . . . His iniquity shall be upon him" (KJV). The Hebrew word "cut off" is a powerful expression, meaning "to be destroyed and consumed utterly; to be cut down." No wonder the Psalmist prayed, "Keep back thy servant also from presumptuous sins; let them not have dominion over me! Then shall I be blameless, and innocent of great transgression" (Ps. 19:13).

No doubt he thought about his great predecessor, Saul, who lost his kingdom through the sin of presumption (1 Sam. 13:8-14).

I reread the story. Saul had sinned in a crucial area. He and Samuel had agreed to meet in Gilgal in seven days. He was under tremendous pressure because the Israeli soldiers were deserting him daily. The blistering heat and the daily taunts of the gargantuan Goliath shook up the troops. The ones who remained were "chicken." They "followed him trembling." The seven days passed for seven years, and when the seventh day came and Samuel didn't show up, Saul was beside himself. His time had run out. There was only one thing to do. He did it. He crossed over the sacred line and presumed to act as priest. He offered the sacrifice preliminary to assuming battle stations. If there was one thing Jews were taught clearly, it was never to transgress the sacred responsibilities of the priests and the Levites. Those God had reserved for a special people and a special time. But Saul caved in. He was afraid his whole army would leave him. So the indignant Samuel greets him with the following words:

"You fool! . . . You have disobeyed the commandment

of the Lord your God. He was planning to make you and your descendants kings of Israel forever, but now your dynasty must end; for the Lord wants a man who will obey him. . ." (1 Sam. 13:13-14a, TLB).

A kingdom lost! A dynasty destroyed! A brave and foolish man lost a golden opportunity because he acted presumptuously. It was a sobering example. But probably the most famous incident of presumption in the history of Israel occurred under Moses' leadership. Moses had sent out the twelve spies into the Promised Land and ten of them came back with a perfectly secular account that was realistic all right, but it was without an iota of faith. Only Caleb and Joshua gave a positive report. The negative confession of the ten was so disconcerting, the people were about to stone Caleb and Joshua for their steadfast conviction that God would still give them the land.

The Lord interposed with His glory and threatened to send a pestilence upon Israel, and to dispossess her in favor of Moses. He offered to make Moses into a nation greater than Israel had ever been. The chance of a lifetime! But not for noble Moses! He pleaded with God and saved their lives and their inheritance. But God was adamant on one point: He utterly refused to let them enter the Promised Land. Only Caleb and Joshua qualified through their faith.

Then the people became contrite, but it was too late; the Lord had already spoken. Now they were all eagerness and courage. "Here we are!" they said. "We realize that we have sinned, but now we are ready to go on into the land the Lord has promised us." Moses was aghast.

He tried to stop them. "It is too late. Now you are disobeying the Lord's orders to return to the wilderness.

Don't go ahead with your plan or you will be crushed by your enemies, for the Lord is not with you'' (Num. 14:41-42, TLB).

But they wouldn't hear, and the sacred record tells us, "But they presumed to go up to the heights. . ." (Num. 14:44) and met disaster. They were beaten from Seir to Hormah (Deut. 1:43-46).

My short study on presumption surprised me. It was painfully clear the Old Testament dealt with it in full. To summarize: (1) Presumption is so deadly that in the majority of cases it was punishable by death. (2) In all but one instance presumption is a sin against God. (3) In most cases, presumption is linked to the word of the Lord. To claim a prophecy to be the word of the Lord, when it was not the word of the Lord, was punishable by death (Deut. 18:20). To overstep the word of the Lord, to go when His word had not come, resulted in destruction (Num. 14:44). But the greatest example of temptation to presumption lay before me. It occurred in the life of Jesus.

2

Early Questions

Why hadn't it worked? What had I done wrong? Had I been unfair in setting a time limit on my healing? Yet it wasn't pausible that such upsetting conditions should continue indefinitely. I had been suffering from a scalp condition. Ugly, gray-white scales fell from my head daily and I was distressed. Although the condition was not particularly painful, it was embarrassing, and I had become a little reluctant to go out in public. Since my shoulders always bore the telltale signs of my condition, a dark suit was particularly revealing. I knew something had to be done, and since I had been newly baptized in the Spirit, I was ready to take action for my healing.

A book that was written by a well-known evangelist had been recommended by my friends. It was radiantly confident that if I followed certain principles, I would be healed. Certainly it was God's will for me to be healed. Wasn't healing in the Atonement? A Jewish rabbi had once pointed out, "If the healing of our physical bodies is not here [referring to Isaiah 53], neither is anything else here."

There is no question but that salvation includes divine healing. Both from the Greek meaning of the word *sodzo* and the commands of Jesus to preach the gospel and to "heal the sick" (Matt. 10:8) it was clear that salvation without healing was incomplete; it was unfinished business. Nor could I doubt the necessity of acting on God's Word, because an act of faith always avails more than a passive receptivity. I knew that Jesus almost always asked for an action on the part of the one in need. "Stretch forth your hands. . . ." "Arise and walk. . . ." "Pick up your bed. . . ." "Go wash your eyes. . . ." I knew positive action was essential for my faith to operate, and so I followed the instructions to a tee.

Every morning I walked into the bathroom where I applied the faith formula assiduously. I showered and brushed my teeth, then I looked squarely into the mirror where my scales were clearly visible. I spoke aloud, exercising my faith.

"Praise God for my healing! Thank you Lord! I praise you for my healing; I praise you for touching those ugly scales." Nothing happened. What was wrong? I checked my faith temperature. It seemed fine. I followed the formula, but nothing worked. "Well," I thought, "maybe God doesn't want to do a gradual healing. Perhaps He is going to do a miracle right before my eyes." Every morning it was the same. Six days went by. If anything, my condition grew worse. I rose with more than my usual enthusiasm on the seventh day. I praised God in faith. Still nothing happened. No miracle, no healing, no visible change. I thought for a while. "Well, really, a week is a small period of time to expect God to work. After all, He is the God of eternity; He can't be hurried. Perhaps I have been trying to box Him in. He is not a man that He should lie (Num. 23:19). I had better give Him another week." So I did. Every morning I arose looking into the mirror and again praised God with faith and fervor proclaiming my healing with complete assurance. After all, it was written—

Things did change. They grew worse. By the end of fourteen days my scalp condition was nearly intolerable. had I skipped part of the procedure? Had I really not truly believed? Was my past catching up to me? I was brought up in the Christian and Missionary Alliance church, a great missionary church that fervently believed in healing. I had heard of a few healings in my earlier days, and my parents rejoiced over a few people who had been healed through prayer. But then college days came and I read a book questioning whether or not healing was in the Atonement. Although the author never really dealt adequately with the exegesis of Isaiah 53 where healing and salvation are both mentioned as being laid on the Messiah, he convinced me through stories of abuse that the great truth of Christ's healing in the Atonement was not operational for today or at least that it seldom occurred.

I remember one story particularly well. The missionary was dying of malaria in Africa, and although quinine was available he refused it. He was entreated by his friends, but he still refused. He was adamant in his faith. He had decided to trust Jesus as his Healer, and that was that! Although he grew weaker and weaker, he still declared his faith. Finally he died. A heroic, but tragic, figure grasping tenaciously to a theology that did not work in the clutch. I was angry and indignant at the unnecessary loss of a precious instrument in the hands of God. If this is what "healing in the Atonement" meant, someone else could have it. It wasn't until years later that I recalled the incident and the fact that from that time on my ardor for healing had cooled considerably. I didn't exactly disbelieve; I simply went into neutral.

But since the Spirit's coming, things had changed for me. I had seen some wonderful healings take place and I had fully expected my own. Of course it wasn't all pure believing. There were moments when I looked at my image in the mirror and fumed, "What are you doing here, you fool? Nothing has happened. Look at those scales. Why don't you go back to your medicine?" But I had decided to tough it out.

A doctor friend had prescribed a medicine that had previously been successful in treating my scalp, and my faith faltered. It would have been so easy to reach for that bottle! What I was doing certainly wasn't working, but I decided against the medicine. After all, the book was pretty clear. It gave the distinct impression that either you trusted God or you used medicine, but not both.

So I persisted for seven more days: "Praise the Lord; thank you, Lord, for my healing. Praise God. I thank you for what you are doing." But I began to feel like a fool. That was the whole trouble; apparently God wasn't doing anything. Try as I could, there were no signs of improvement. The fourteenth day came and went; the scalp condition was nearly intolerable. Finally, feeling horribly guilty, I reached for the bottle. Within a week the condition had cleared. I was sure God had not deserted me, but such a conclusion was tentative and guilt-ridden. Why couldn't God use medicine as well as prayer? Yet I carried the uneasy conviction that I had settled for second best. I reviewed the argument once more. Healing is as much in the Atonement as is salvation. As everyone who calls on the name of the Lord is saved, why is it not equally true that everyone who asks for healing is healed? Where were the holes in the argument? What had gone wrong? Had I fallen for a gimmick? Hadn't I tried the formula? A formula ought to work every time. Or was healing after all not reducible to a formula? There was the real question. Perhaps I had even been exercising a general faith in God, a kind of faith without certain knowledge, which worked some of the time, but not all the time. Had I tried to apply as a universal truth something that really belonged more to the realm of general faith?

Why hadn't my faith worked? I had exercised my faith to stand on God's Word. I had prayed the prayer of faith, I had resisted doubt, and I did not consult a doctor. What had gone wrong? Slowly an idea formed. It grew into a tentative conclusion that has since become a settled conviction. Healing is such a complex business that no one but God really has the answers. Humility is the way to understanding and we will never know it all. "God is greater than man" (Job 33:12).

It took me many years to mature to the conviction that the God of infinite variety has many different ways of healing, but all are evidences of His providential grace. Reflecting on the life of Jesus helped me to see this. Some could have claimed it was more spiritual to be healed simply by His Word, while others could argue that to use spittle—considered by many of that time to have medicinal value—was an aid to the blind man's faith, a point of contact, but was equally spiritual. Some could claim that when Jesus healed instantaneously it was more honoring to God than when it took several trips to the pool (John 9). But as I reflected on why Jesus used so many different ways to heal, the question was answered in the asking. What does it matter how He healed? The point is He did heal and He is the source of all healing. If God is the source of all healing and Jesus is our model for today, why can we not accept medical science and healing by prayer as equally provided by our Father's loving care? Why should we send millions of sincere, Spirit-filled Christians on a guilt trip for using medicine when medicine is also part of God's great healing plan? Could we not bring relief to millions of guilt-ridden people by the simple words, "Now, see here, Jesus is the source of all healing; if He chooses to use medicine one time, and prayer the next, is He not equally our benefactor in both cases?"

When, ten years before, I had been in Scotland completing my Ph.D. in theology at the University of Edinburgh, a sort of Presbyterian Annapolis, I had met a strangely gifted Presbyterian minister at one of my classes. I invited him home. He was speaking about a gift of healing God had given to him and I was astonished. I wasn't even sure how many of the Church of Scotland ministers had had a personal encounter with Christ, and here was this astute and educated minister speaking in an offhand manner about many remarkable healings that had occurred in his ministry. I sat enthralled. In fact I couldn't understand why news of this great gift had not spread over Scotland. Now I suspect his congregation suppressed the news as much as possible with that good Scottish reserve. After all, such a thing simply wasn't done. I began to think about my own ills. I had a bad back that drove me up a wall when I failed to sleep on a hard surface. To this day I put a board under the sheet or bed pad, in order to maintain a healthy back, but I really wanted my back healed. After all, it's not very convenient hauling a board all over the world with you wherever you go.

I also used glasses for reading. In fact, I had done so for many years. So I thought, there is no harm in trying. He had an absolute faith. I believed in a general way in healing and I wanted to be healed. I have never seen anybody pray as he did before or since that time. I remember that little Scottish living room so well. My dear landlady, Mrs. Laurie, now since departed to be with the Lord, was sitting in silent amazement in one corner. My roommate, Stuart Merriam, later to be the dynamic founder of Highland Mission in New Guinea, was dubious about the whole business, but I was game to try. What did I have to lose? He ran his fingers over the afflicted area, much as my chiropractor runs his electrical machine over my back to detect the troubled areas. He ran his fingers lightly from the top of my spine down to the end, and then he snapped his fingers as though he were cracking a whip. I wondered why; he never did explain.

Then he prayed for my eyes with the same technique. Hands lightly placed on my eyes, he prayed a soft and simple believing prayer: "Lord Jesus, heal your servant, heal his eyes." And then, gently moving his hands, he would snap them as he reached the edges of my eyes. Although his hands were pleasant enough, and I felt strange stirrings within, it took many years for the early stirrings to erupt into a beautiful, new language of prayer.

Strange to relate, my back remained the same, but my eyes were wondrously healed. My healing had come in spite of myself. I didn't even know I should no longer use my glasses, so I continued to read with them. My dissertation completed, I returned to the United States and began working with the Navigators in a warm relationship that lasted several years. Since the Navigators don't want their trainees to start in too exalted a condition, my first job was helping to dig the grave of Dawson Trotman, founder of the Navigators. After a couple of weeks of grave digging (the ground was unbelievably hard), I was promoted to the grounds crew where I got to rake leaves and rocks. However, my true talents as a house painter became known, and soon I was the highest man on the glen, painting from the towering third story of the beautiful castle General Palmer had built. It was after this last promotion that the accident happened. A lovely young lady, Mary Noyes, affectionately known as Happy Racket, was sitting in an old Buick sedan someone had loaned me after we had shared a ministry together. She sat on the glasses and they smashed into a million pieces. I was disturbed and disconsolate because of my financial condition.

"Lord, I'm too broke to get them repaired. I've got to read. What do I do?" I had completely forgotten the healing prayer, and I really don't remember any special impression, but with no other alternatives in the offing, I started to read without glasses. To my amazement, the letters stood out clear and distinctly—God had healed me! It was a turning point in my life. Gone was the skepticism and unbelief. I knew God could heal. I had the proof—He had healed me! But I also learned something else. It was not my faith but God's sovereign love that healed me.

It wasn't until I was well over forty that I began using glasses again. Ophthalmologists tell us that after forty the natural aging process catches up with us, and we can expect to wear glasses.

But my back remained the same. What was I to make of this? If proper faith was the only ingredient, as the book on healing insisted, why were my eyes healed, and my back was not? Was there a possibility my faith had slipped when he prayed for my back? But that didn't really add up since both healing prayers took place within a few seconds of each other. Nor was it true to my experience to assume that in one instance I had exercised perfect faith, and the other instance, no faith at all. It was puzzling.

What were the variables? Was there any way to discover them and adapt myself accordingly so that healing always occurred? Is it true that a person's faith is the sole factor in healing? If so, why had God so wondrously healed in one situation, and not in the other two? The mystery was just beginning. It was to deepen considerably before I had any satisfactory answers.

3

From the Pinnacle
of the Temple

How *do* you tell the difference between bold faith and
foolish presumption? Are there no safeguards against
presumption? How can you help people understand what
presumption is without destroying their faith?

"My task is to build faith, not annihilate it," I said to
myself.

Yet it is absolutely clear, both from Scripture and
practical experience, that presumption exists and that it's
to be avoided like the plague. "Lord," I complained,
"writing a book on the difference between faith and
presumption is no snap. I'm not even sure I know the
difference. If I can't understand it myself, how can I
explain it to others?" I waited. Nothing happened.
Gradually, I began to realize God wanted me to *think* it
through. But He wanted me to use a particular kind of
thinking, *faith thinking*. The kind that does not destroy,
but builds true faith. Old Anselm had it right. What is

theology but "faith in search of understanding"? Certainly one has to begin with faith; otherwise his theological search has no real starting point. But Anselm was driven by the knowledge that God wanted him to love Him with all his mind as well as his heart, hence the search to understand.

"One man's faith is another man's presumption" appears to be an axiomatic statement. Yet, what works for me may not work for someone else. The stories of men who ventured out on faith and were greatly rewarded are legion. Dawson Trotman, founder of the Navigators, was a man known for his faith. One day with little or no money he set out with a team of men to cross the country holding gospel rallies and exhorting Christians to get into the Word. They had a wondrously successful ministry, and God met all their needs. What jubilation when they returned!

My friend, Ken Swan, was a great admirer of Trotman. He was a tall, lanky young man with an engaging smile, and a penchant for the simple life. Eventually Ken found himself owning and operating a small farm "far from the madding crowd's ignoble strife." He wanted to follow the Lord in simple faith as well. So, he started up his old car with a full tank of gas and plenty of faith and drove mile after mile. His ministry was a smashing success until the old car stopped. It had run out of gas. No amount of prayer made it work. No miraculous supply of gasoline extended the mileage he could get. No hitchhikers appeared who turned out to be "angels unawares." No strangers came pressing money on him from out of the crowd. Nothing. Why did it work for Dawson and not for him? Dawson moved across the country under God's daily provision. Ken tried it and ran out of gas. Was Dawson more holy than he and thus a better recipient of God's grace? The questions seemed ridiculous. If Christ saved both Dawson and Ken, surely both must have a measure of faith. But Ken and I both learned a valuable lesson from his experience. One man's faith really is, indeed, another man's presumption.

Presumption is such a universal possibility that even our Lord was tempted by it. If out of the great arsenal of temptation weapons Satan had to choose from, he chose presumption, there must be a reason. Presumption is a sin that particularly tempts bold, courageous men of faith who are eager to accomplish something for God. If even Jesus were tempted by the sin of presumption, then surely it was a possibility for us all. Actually, I've always been bothered by the notion that Jesus could be tempted by a sin the Old Testament considered so deadly, for He was one of the authors of the Old Testament law. Could He break His own law? Yet, when I took down my Bible and read again that story in Matthew 4:5-11, it was impossible to deny.

> Then the devil took him to the holy city, and set him on the pinnacle of the temple. (v. 5)

I had been near that site many times. Towering 170 feet above the gorge of Kidron, the pinnacle of the temple was probably the most conspicuous spot in all of Jerusalem. Herod's magnificent temple was covered with sheets of gold that made it one of the most spectacular buildings in the ancient world. It was easy to envision Jesus with His white garments fluttering against tha. dark blue Israeli sky in this inaccessible but highly visible spot. It would have been impossible to have stood there long without great hordes of people looking up. Even today, throngs of visitors glue their eyes to the Mosque of Omar where the ancient temple stood. It has been estimated that in Jesus' day as many as 2,000,000 people celebrated Passover in Jerusalem. It would have been hard to find a better launching pad for an instantaneous miracle ministry. The devil was direct and to the point:

> "If you are the Son of God, throw yourself down; for it is written, 'He will give his angels charge of you' and 'On their hands they will bear you up lest you strike your foot against a stone.' " (Matt. 4:6)

If Jesus had jumped, and had lived, it would have been a fantastic miracle, proof positive that God was with Him. Jesus could not have been unaware of the crowds milling around below pointing Him out, chattering excitedly. Perhaps many a mother had to answer her child's human fly instincts. "Mom, how did He get up there? Can I climb up too?" But mothers, too, wondered if this could be the promised Son of David, the Messiah.

The devil had played a trump card. He presented Jesus with a bona fide shortcut to success. Jesus could have gained instantaneous recognition as the great miracle-worker. Nothing could have stopped Him. The people would gladly have recognized Him as Messiah. His kingdom would have been a cinch. A man who could swoop up and down like an eagle could no doubt drive

Rome from Jerusalem, and that was what the people wanted more than anything else. An instant Messiah! An instant kingdom! What an opportunity!

In the previous temptation, Satan had tempted Jesus with bread. Since Jesus had had nothing to eat for forty days, it was a natural enough temptation. Jesus had answered Satan with Scripture, probably to give us an example or, perhaps, to remind *himself* that true protection was His, only as long as He stood upon the Word. So Satan considers, "Aha! Jesus' strong point is Scripture. Well, I know a few verses myself; two can play at that game."

His strategy was clear. If he could get Jesus to launch out on a single Bible passage with no special word from the Father, *he would destroy the Son of God*. His words were uncannily clever. "If you are the Son of God. . . ." Most men rise immediately to defend their own understanding of themselves and their mission. This was the second time Satan had challenged Jesus. "Jesus, if you are the Son of God . . . ." His argument was rational enough. In essence he was saying, "Jesus, you want to help people. You want to change things for the better. There is a fast way to gain their allegiance, a shortcut to your cherished ambition. Let men see this great miracle, how God favors you, and you will win the world to the side of goodness and truth. Defy the laws of gravity, that is, if you really are the one you say you are, and God will take care of you. I can even prove it from the Bible." And he quoted Psalm 91:11-12. Almost, that is. But what he left out was crucial. It was a single phrase. In fact, a phrase so insignificant that I missed it several times before I came to really see it. The phrase he omitted—not wanting to remind Jesus—was: "to guard you in all your ways" (Ps. 91:11b). In other words, in the ordinary business of life, the angels do guard you, but that gives you no right to go steeple hopping! By omitting the exact quotation, and by misapplying the verse, Satan made this a presumptuous act. "Just cast yourself down and trust God."

I asked myself what would have happened if He had. Of course, this is not a real question, because Jesus did not succumb to the temptation, but we have to live with the possibility that Jesus could have perished if He had hurled himself down. Furthermore, I can hear a scoffer's sneer in Satan's words, "If thou be the Son of God . . . ." *God never performs miracles to prove He is God. God performs miracles to meet the needs of His people and for His own glory.*

Now what was Jesus' response? Jesus continued to quote Scripture. "Again it is written 'You shall not tempt the Lord your God' " (Matt. 4:7). Jesus didn't go off half-cocked on one verse of Scripture. Had He wanted to establish a cult, He would have used that method. But Jesus was establishing the kingdom of God, and He knew better than to try to build it on some isolated verse, distorted out of context.

One of the great truths of Reformation theology is not only "must it be written," but "on the other hand," must be written also. We need the whole counsel of God for doctrine.

Scripture is like a gyroscope, those wonderful little self-balancing mechanisms which, when wound up tightly, can be cocked to one side as they spin, yet never falter or fall. They just keep turning in perfect synchronization. This is the beauty of Scripture. Scripture compared with Scripture gives a self-balancing power to keep the believer from the fallacy of building doctrines on one verse.

"No one has the right," Jesus says, "to put God presumptuously to the test—*not even the Son of God*. No one has the right to force God's hand." The Father was silent and the Son did not presume. In this case, presumption was to take the general provision of God's Word and make it apply to a specific situation where God had not spoken.

There is a vast difference between tempting God and proving God. Israel went through the Red Sea, proving God. The Egyptians did exactly the same thing, and they died for their presumption. What was the difference? Israel heard a word from God; Egypt did not.

Israel moved forward at the spoken word of God, but God did not speak to the Egyptians. When they moved, they perished.

There is a difference between the Word of God in general and the word of God which is spoken specifically to you. In the Greek New Testament this is sometimes expressed by two different words for "word": *logos* and *rhema*.

Logos denotes the expression of thought, not the mere name of an object, but the body, conception, or an idea, like God.[1] In other words, we may think of *logos* as a sort of universal, at least in the Gospel of John. A universal is something which is existent everywhere and under all conditions. *Logos* is the Gospel, the Ten Commandments, the sum total of God's utterances. They are true everywhere and under all conditions. It is God's speech,

His discourse.

The differences and similarities in the usages of *logos* and *rhema* are enormously complex. However there is little support for the idea of one scholar that the "words are more or less synonymous." In John, at least, *rhema* was a specific statement whereas *logos* tended to be general. *Rhema* was more precise and definite. The particular is *rhema*. When a universal is needed, *logos* is used.

Four usages appear in John. First, the *rhema* represents individual words, while *logos* is the universal. A second usage employs *logos* in the plural, "You are not hearing my words, i.e., my messages." Thirdly, Jesus states, "I have proclaimed my *logos* to you." Here His *logos* is His whole message. The fourth usage is unique to John. Here Jesus becomes the *logos*, the final Word of God.[2]

Thus, the ultimate meaning of *logos* is the incarnate Word of God, Jesus Christ. He is the Word which ends all words. "Jesus Christ the same yesterday, and to day, and for ever" (Heb. 13:8, KJV). There He is—Jesus—God's last Word to man. The eternal Word of the eternal God. There—in Jesus—the Word of God took final and absolute form. Who is the Word of God? Jesus is the Word of God. Whether anyone in the world believes or not, Jesus is the *logos*, the Word of God objectified, the personal Word, the unlimited Son of God. W.E. Vine says, "He is the reality and totality of human nature. His was the Shekinah glory in open manifestation. 'The only begotten Son which is in the bosom of the Father, He has declared Him.' Thus the Word *logos* is the personal manifestation, not a part of divine nature, but of the whole Deity."[3]

"In several passages in the writings of John, the *logos*

denotes the essential Word of God, i.e., the personal (hypostatic) wisdom and power in union with God, His minister in the creation and government of the universe, the cause of all the world's life both physical and ethical, which for the procurement of man's salvation put on human nature in the person of Jesus the Messiah and shone forth conspicuously from His words and deeds. . . ."[4]

Glory! In other words, the eternal God became flesh, clothed with manhood, to win our eternal salvation! Surely this is the loftiest use of *logos* in the history of literature; the Word was God!

Sometimes it is a word from the Lord, delivered with His authority and made effective by His power (Acts 10:36). Sometimes it also refers to doctrine (Matt. 13:20). In other words, when we look at Jesus as the *logos*, we see Him not just as a part of God, but as an expression of the whole deity of God. This was the wonder of Jesus, that the Shekinah of the Old Testament, which was rarely beheld and never seen in its full glory, was fully revealed to us in the Son, Jesus.

Rhema, on the other hand, often denotes that which is spoken, what is uttered in speech or in writing, particularly in John. It is not necessarily divine (Matt. 12:36). It is often a word spoken for a particular occasion, the "now" word of God. The emphasis with *rhema* is not on the thought nor on its objective quality, nor is it as all-inclusive as the word *logos*, but the emphasis is on the actual word spoken. Sometimes it is a word that is heard and then acted upon as in Acts 13:42. It is a word a man takes action on. It is a personal word. "The word is nigh thee, even in thy mouth, and in thy heart" (Rom. 10:8,

KJV). Here the word *rhema* is used.

Many of us heard the gospel many times before we responded to it. When we heard the gospel, was it not *logos* the first time we heard it? Of course, it was. But as we listened, the Holy Spirit brought increasing conviction to us and one wonderful day it became *rhema* to us. No longer just the "Word" but now a "word to us." That was the day we may have gone forward and suddenly the *logos* of God, eternal and uncompromising, became Jesus' wonderful word of comfort and freedom to us. That was when the *logos* became *rhema*. This is precisely what Romans 10:17 means: "So then faith cometh by hearing, and hearing *by the word* [rhema] *of God*" (KJV). You see, in that wonderful moment of conversion we heard and *acted* upon the Word. Then the *logos* became *rhema* and we were saved.

Sometimes *rhema* is a special occasion word. It is a particular word spoken to us. It finds us in our need. In Ephesians 6:17, when Paul speaks of the sword of the Spirit as the word of God, he uses *rhema*. In other words, it is not the whole Bible, which some people use as a bludgeon, but a particular word for a particular occasion. We all know people who use the Word as a club: "I've got a word for you, brother." Bang! Remember the pastor who stood before his people and said, "I am the good shepherd, I beat my sheep."

Paul makes the illustrations graphic. Here are two warriors all set for battle. Both have on their headgear, breastplates and protection for their feet. Both hold a shield in their left hands. Both stand at warriors' stance. But there the similarities cease.

One is armed with a sword, but the other has only a club. He wields it above his head. He swooshes it through the air. His foe deftly deflects it by using his shield. He whirls it around again. Another miss. He never connects with his foe and he is getting tired. Sweat pours down his face. He wheezes and blows. He is bewildered and perplexed. Hasn't he used the Word?

Paul calls from the sidelines, "Not a club, you dummy! Use it as a sword!"

All too many use clubs when they should be using swords. The Spirit knows how to adjust the proper word for a maximum thrust. That is why it's called the "sword of the Spirit." It is not our sword. It is the Spirit's sword. No wonder Paul uses *rhema*, the word used for a special occasion to show us how to win in battle. It is the word the Spirit carefully chooses which accomplishes the work.

Rhema is not always divine in origin. It often denotes a word that is spoken so a particular action can be taken. When the Bible speaks of idle words being accounted for, it uses *rhema*.

In John 1 *logos* is divine, while *rhema* may be a human word. The *logos* tends to be universal, while the *rhema* is often used in the particular sense. The *logos* is objective, while the *rhema* is often subjective, a word spoken for a particular occasion to a particular person. The *logos* is eternal, while the *rhema* is often contemporary. This means that when we look at the Word of God, and what the Word has to say about God, we must be careful to distinguish between the *rhema*, the word which is spoken for that particular occasion, and the *logos*, the word which is eternal.

This is graphically illustrated in the story John relates about himself and Peter, toward the end of Jesus' life on earth.

Peter had just been told how he was going to end his life and he was concerned about John—for no word of suffering had been spoken about him. Was he to get off this planet scot-free? "Lord, what about this man?" In other words, "What's going to happen to my friend, John?" Jesus answered, "If it's my will that he remain until I come, what is that to you? Follow me" (John 21:20-22). Here is a clear-cut example of Jesus, the shepherd, establishing a relationship with both of His sheep, to follow Him without question. Peter is one sheep. His job is to follow. John is also a sheep. His job is to follow. In other words, Jesus is saying, "Peter, I have a *rhema* for you and I have a *rhema* for John, but the *rhema* I have for John is none of your business." One of the best qualities of a sheep is that he knows his master's voice. Jesus is saying, "I want each of my sheep to be in such an intimate relationship with me, to be so personally related, that they will not only hear *logos*, the general Word of God, but that they will hear the *rhema*, the particular word which I have to speak to them."

At the same time it is essential to remember Jesus never intended any of His sheep to surrender their capacity to hear His voice to any other shepherd. Even the newest lamb needs to learn how to follow the shepherd's voice.

When we fail to discern the difference between *logos* and *rhema*, trouble comes. Proverbs 13:10 says, "Through presumption comes nothing but strife. But with those who receive counsel is wisdom" (NAS).

Working on the widely taught premise which states, "We always receive what we say or confess," it didn't take my friend Tom long to conclude that a positive prayer of faith would always heal. Tom had been a friend of mine for many years, although he was often beset by longstanding anxieties. Recently baptized in the Spirit he took a new lease on life, and as part of his new understanding he adopted the familiar theological stance that "confession brings possession." To him, faith was all that was necessary. Healing was simply an exercise of that faith.

He heard of a young child dying of leukemia. Bursting with enthusiasm and new confidence in God's healing power, he and some of his friends went to the home of the child. "May we come in and pray for your child?" The parents cordially invited him in. After explaining the wonderful message of Christ's great healing power, they followed the pattern established in James 5 for the healing of the sick. They anointed the child with oil, prayed the prayer of faith, and left, but not before Tom spoke some words that were to come back to haunt him for many days. He said to the anxious parents, "There's no doubt about it, the child will be healed. There is not a thing to worry about or to be anxious about. God has spoken in His Word; it's got to be true, so continue to confess the healing; it's bound to come."

He left, rejoicing, absolutely confident that his prayer had been answered. A few days later, however, the child was dead. My friend Tom went into a spiritual tailspin. Wasn't God's promise in the Word? Did it not say that healing was present for us? Why hadn't God healed the child? It was *logos*, indeed, that Tom acted upon; but it had not become *rhema* to him. It was legal, but it was not experiential. Tom learned there was a great difference between the legal provision and the experiential, existential appropriation.

A lack of knowledge of this difference, I'm afraid, dooms many Spirit-filled people to premature death. I know of a young lady who could possibly die shortly of breast cancer because she believes confession is possession, and she steadfastly refuses the necessary operation. I wonder how many other women in America are needlessly dying from breast cancer because they've taken someone's word, that *confession brings possession*, without any specific word from the Lord themselves.

A fine Lutheran family in my colleague Howard Ervin's church was in a state of consternation. A tumor had appeared on the cleft palate of their little girl. They did what any of us would have done; they took her to the church for prayer. Perhaps those who prayed were very new in the Spirit; perhaps they did not recognize the sensitivity of the little girl, but at any rate the damage was done. I am certain they prayed with the best intentions in the world, but their theology had a tragic effect on the little girl. "We have prayed in faith for your healing. Now you're healed. All you need to do is to confess your healing and in time you will possess it." In fact, though, she did not grow better, but rather, worse. Her mind tormented her. "I didn't have the faith because I'm growing worse. That is why Jesus does not love me." Her spiritual trauma became so great she would not even allow calm and collected Howard to pray for her. In her child's mind prayer was where she discovered that God did not love her. They had told her she was healed by faith. All she had to do was "exercise her faith." But in fact she was not healed; therefore, she did not exercise faith. That was why God did not love her.

Shortly afterwards they moved to the Midwest, where a competent surgeon confirmed their worst fears. He said to the parents, "I'm sorry, but your daughter will have to have surgery."

The family was devastated. The little girl was stricken with guilt and remorse. If only she'd had the necessary faith! Jesus would then have loved her enough to heal her! But she had already tried so hard.

When they related the story to their new Lutheran pastor, he remarked, "They have turned the ministry of healing into a ministry of condemnation."

Sincerity is no substitute for truth. The parachutist who clawed his way through his leather jacket, his shirt and his tee shirt in search of the rip cord on the wrong side was doubtless sincere, but he was still dead wrong. Nor is sincerity proof against presumption. Some of the most sincere people in the world are presumptuous, and as Jesus pointed out it is utter folly to tempt the Lord (Matt. 4:7).

There is a remarkably close connection between presumption and pride. In fact, it is safe to say that pride is the basis of presumption; the words are identical in Hebrew. The word *zadon* means arrogance, pride, insolence or presumption. In Proverbs 13:10 the KJV is translated "only by pride cometh contention: but with the well advised is wisdom." The NAS translates the same word as "presumption." The Psalmist prayed, "Keep back thy servant from presumptuous sins" (Ps. 19:13). He was well aware of the consequences.

Strange as it may seem, a person may know the will of God, attempt to perform it and still be presumptuous. You may recall David's bringing up of the ark from Kirjath-jearim. There all Israel gathered to honor the ark and praise the Lord. Naturally they wanted the ark to have the best, so they put it on a new cart and the whole occasion of bringing back the ark became a jubilant celebration. All the people danced, sang and shouted before the Lord, worshiping and praising God.

Suddenly disaster struck. Somebody from the street department had goofed. The cart hit a pothole that threatened to discharge the ark. Naturally the driver reached back to save his precious cargo but he had no sooner reached around to stabilize the ark than he was struck dead. David was fearful, horrified, and angry. What had gone wrong? Didn't God want the ark brought back? Why had God killed this poor man when he only wanted to help? David was so terrified that for three months he left the ark at the house of Obed-edom, where it greatly prospered him and his family.

In the meantime David did his homework and discovered that he had acted presumptuously. He found out that God's will must be executed by God's man in God's way and in God's time. All three factors are of tremendous importance. David was the right man and his timing was right but he had used the wrong method. Only priests were permitted to carry the ark, so he called the priests together and said to them, "You are the heads of the fathers' houses of the Levites; sanctify yourselves, you and your brethren, so you may bring up the ark of the Lord, the God of Israel, to the place that I have prepared for it. Because you did not carry it the first time, the Lord our God broke forth upon us, because we did not care for it in the way that is ordained" (1 Chron. 15:12-13; see also 1 Chron. 13). David discovered a classic principle of the believer's walk: *Divine ardor is no substitute for divine order.*

For us the presumption is more often in the timing than in the call. We have a vision from God. We really receive an authentic understanding of what He wants accomplished, but in nine times out of ten we make our mistake in the timing. Ecclesiastes 8:5 says, ". . . the mind of a wise man will know the time and the way."

Timing also plays a large part in healing. I believe the time will come when healing will be as universal as salvation; that is, that as all who call upon the Name of the Lord are saved, so all who will call upon the Name of the Lord shall be healed. But that time is not yet fully come and the Scripture is clear—the "wise man knows the time and the way." The kingdom is not yet fully come. It is still in the process of realization. In a limited sense it is here and truly here, but only in part. Its final realization awaits our Lord's return. We may liken the benefits of the Atonement to one of the new, super cold pills that boasts it releases its medication at properly spaced intervals. In our dispensation, salvation is universal for all who sincerely repent and receive Christ as Lord and Savior. I have yet to meet a man or woman who sincerely called upon the Name of the Lord who was not saved. But I have met many godly saints who have called upon the Lord but have not been healed. The time release for that particular medication from the Atonement has evidently not yet been universally released. In fact, it is quite possible that full and universal healing may not come until the millenium. The kingdom is "here and now" and yet "not yet." As Jeremias suggests, it is still in the process of realization. The "not yet" of the kingdom may only come fully at Christ's return.

On the other hand, when God does speak a *rhema,* a true word to you, you can bet your life on it.

When a true word from God comes, it doesn't only happen sometimes; it happens all the time. When the Lord really speaks a word to our hearts it is something which is essentially unshakable. That kind of knowledge is really more secure than knowledge by reason, experience or any other form. It is knowledge which is divinely given. It is knowledge which takes us beyond the realm of usual knowing into a realm in which the knowing cannot be doubted. As Oral Roberts often says, "I know that I know that I know that I know." It may be called pneumatic knowledge—knowledge by the Spirit.

One day I had the privilege of experiencing this kind of knowing. A fine young faculty wife at Oral Roberts University was particularly close to my wife, Jo Ann. She had experienced a few problems and therefore was being examined by the physician. She had taken an EKG and the cardiogram showed no problem, but when she walked the treadmill the heart doctor, considered by many one of the finest in Tulsa, was firm.

"Ruth, there's no question but that there is an obstruction in one of the vessels leading to your heart. It will be necessary for us to do an angiogram in order to find out the extent of the obstruction." The doctor fell silent, then continued, "I have to tell you that the angiogram can in itself produce a heart attack. However, we have a contingency plan. If it does, we will go to one of your legs, strip a vein there, put it into your chest and thereby hope to by-pass the obstruction."

Ruth thought for a long moment and as the sinister truth gradually sank in she said, "Doctor, are you telling me that it is possible that I have only one day left to live?"

The doctor did not soften the blow. He responded, "I'm sorry, but that's the way the cookie crumbles."

With these encouraging words ringing in her ears, she called my wife in a near panic. As soon as Jo Ann mentioned the problem to me, God spoke a word to my spirit. I immediately responded with words totally out of character: "Honey, she's going to be okay." I was astonished as I listened to what I was saying. I don't know how I knew. I only knew that I knew. And I had ample opportunity over the next few hours to test that word very carefully. That evening Jo Ann and I visited Ruth and her husband, Frank, at their house. We prayed together, felt refreshed in the Spirit, and believed for a great miracle from God.

After we had finished the evening and she had told me the whole story, she looked me straight in the eyes. "Chuck," she asked, "do you still believe that I will be okay?"

I was surprised at my own audacity and boldness, but questioning the response of the Spirit within, though my mind was dubious too, I could truthfully say to her, "Ruth, you will be okay."

The next day President Oral Roberts went over to see

her. He, too, confirmed the good news. He prayed for her and as he listened to the Spirit he gave her the word that God gave him. He said to her, "Ruth, there may have been something wrong, but it is now completely healed." Ruth was reassured, but she still had to go to the hospital. The night before the operation Jo Ann and I, independently, kept waking through the night. Each time we awakened we found ourselves interceding in prayer for Ruth. It was something divinely given by the Spirit. Neither of us had planned it that way.

At eight o'clock in the morning when the angiogram was to take place, I had a strange experience. I almost felt that the tube which had to be inserted in the groin to take the necessary pictures had actually been inserted in my groin instead. I seemed to feel its actual presence. An almost physical panic occurred in me as the tube seemed to advance toward my heart. I don't explain it but I know from others that often those who intercede do sometimes come to such a point of empathy that they are able to feel what the other person is feeling. I had specifically prayed that Ruth would feel no sense of fear when the angiogram took place, and now in her stead I actually felt the edges of panic myself. I can't explain such things. I can only report them, but the results were tremendous.

After checking in every way possible, the doctor called and said, "Ruth, we've taken x-rays of every part of your heart and I am glad to tell you there is absolutely no obstruction at all." He had no explanation, but he went on to say, "You are perfectly healthy. There is no restriction on your diet, there is no restriction on your exercise habits. You are as good as new!"

That's what happens when the *rhema* is combined with intercessory prayer. In this beautiful miracle, God acted in a supernatural way, but only after He had spoken a *rhema* to me. It wasn't simply on the basis of a *logos,* but it was a special word spoken for that specific incident. You say, Chuck, how do you know? Well, I can't really tell you how I knew, but I did know and certainly the results confirmed it. When it's a true *rhema* the results will always confirm God's word to you, and be confirmed by the resulting action.

This wasn't the kind of faith I could work up. I didn't sing twenty-nine verses of "Only Believe" so that my faith could get built up to the place where I could venture out and believe. It was a pure gift from God. In fact, probably three miracles were involved. God gave me the miracle of faith, a word of knowledge, and then His miracle healing power took place. We may discover that many times these three miracles go hand in hand.

On the other hand, we have no control over this special word from God. Another friend of mine was suffering from the same problem. He was a fine dentist in the city and was diagnosed as having a major obstruction in his heart as well. An operation seemed imminent.

Again, I went before the Lord. I searched out my own heart and spirit and earnestly prayed that God would heal him as miraculously as He had healed Ruth. There was no answering word in my heart. I had no assurance in my spirit that it would take place. But I wanted to believe. I tried to believe. I attempted to exercise my faith, but I could not bring myself to say to him, "Al, you have no problem, God has spoken a word to me," because God simply had not spoken. To have done so would have been presumptuous and perhaps disastrous.

Al went through his operation and God healed, but it was a different kind of healing. Al has had the finest recovery of anyone I know from such a delicate and difficult operation. He is as healthy a specimen as you would want to see, but it came by a different channel. Was it not the same God who healed in both cases but by a different means? Ultimately is it not true that all real healing is from God?

The Whole Counsel

One of the principles that guides us in appraising doctrine or teaching is not only the presence of isolated verses to support a particular teaching, but a much more difficult question, "What does the Scripture as a whole teach?" For example, teachings in the Old Testament seem to support polygamy, at least by example, but when I look at the Scriptures as a whole I find that monogamy is rooted in the original creation story, reaffirmed by Jesus and taught by the apostle Paul. In other words, when we look at the Bible as a whole, interpreted Christologically—that is, when we focus on the person, sayings and deeds of Jesus of Nazareth—we find that monogamy is the clear intent of Scripture. We use the word "Christologically" for a very good reason. Jesus is Lord of all, even the Scriptures. Since the body cannot be above the head, Christ's lordship extends over the whole of Scripture. It is the final lordship and that means that what Christ teaches, the Church also must teach. The

Church cannot take its doctrine from certain isolated Scriptures and build its case for polygamy, baptism for the dead, plural marriage, or anything else, without seeing how that particular doctrine coincides with the totality of the teachings of Jesus and the apostles. This is what I mean by referring all doctrine finally to Christ.

Whenever the Church or a segment of the Church takes a particular teaching or truth of the Bible and detaches it from its relation to the total truth, pushing it to its logical extreme, it inevitably results in heresy. Heresy is not latent paganism. Heresy is truth distorted, exaggerated to an intolerable extreme. It is truth out of focus, out of balance with the whole. In fact, one might say the whole secret of good doctrine is caught up in that beautiful word—balance. Over the years I have come to realize what a magnificent word it really is and how hard it is to come by! It is very tough work—staying in balance—because it not only means constant comparison of Scripture with Scripture; it also means a constant review of our theological pride and presumption in thinking that we alone have the right answers. Not only do our heads have to be right in order to have a proper theology, but so do our hearts. And it is infinitely harder to guard our hearts than our heads!

For example, I was blessed by the Lord with a beautiful encounter with the Holy Spirit. He enriched my life in many ways. I was eager to share it. The pages of the New Testament were no longer the dusty pages of what once had been a history I longed for but could not find. It had become a living reality to me.

I saw people miraculously healed by God, just as they

were in Jesus' day, and scores set free from the bondage of demonic spirits. And I found myself raised to a new level of worship and joy that I had never known before. I found a new kind of fellowship too, a loving fellowship with Spirit-filled friends that I simply did not know existed. At times the love level rose so high in those meetings that I would have been perfectly willing to empty out my wallet for total strangers and hug people I had never found huggable before. There was an amazing new liberty and freedom in prayer. I enjoyed the sense of devotion and praise that came through the use of my prayer language, and although it was never an ecstatic experience, as so many seem to think, it did bring me into a new intimacy with the Lord Jesus. For me it was a new way of living, a new dimension, which had definitely entered my life and filled it with power. I tried desperately to stay submissive to the authorities God had placed over me, but it seemed people didn't understand. God had become a 'now' God to me. What to me had become a new way of enjoying God and His wonderful, surprising contemporaneity was for my peers and associates an alarming evidence that "Chuck has gotten off the track," and that, "The tongues movement has taken him in."

What was I to do? The more I insisted on the benefits to my personal life of devotion and tried to prove my point from the Bible and history, the more obstinate they became! How could they be so blind and stupid? They had never been that way before. Now, suddenly, Chuck, one of the fair-haired boys, became Chuck, the spiritual leper. Some of my friends traveled miles just to get around me.

Those who had asked to hear about what God had done for me decided they didn't really want to hear after all. I was hiding something if I didn't share and I was pushing something when I did. No matter what I did, it wasn't right. While rumors and reports spread everywhere, I spent a good share of my time trying to put out brush fires, and as soon as I got one put out another broke out someplace else. I began to think I was a fireman.

What was wrong with my case? I could prove I was right from Scripture. Didn't the apostles enjoy the charismata? Wasn't Paul the one who thanked God he spoke in tongues "more than you all" (1 Cor. 14:18)? And no doubt about it, I had had an experience. But the response of my friends produced a fleshly reaction in me. History showed us that charismata existed. Theology acknowledged it; it was clearly taught. The Bible taught it. That should have settled it. But it didn't. Exegesis was with me. How could I be wrong? I was right. I was "right" enough to be wrong. I was trying to establish the authenticity of my experience and I had the goods theologically, historically and experience-wise. But my friends weren't hearing theology or experience. They were hearing something else. "Chuck has a new experience. He wants us all to have it. He used to be a humble guy, but now he thinks he's got something we haven't got. He's better than we are."

Roles reversed just the other day for me. The shoes changed feet. I was enraptured by the brilliant conversation of my new friend, a diplomat of international standing. He was a genuine genius type, almost universal in his knowledge and scope. In his field he really knew his onions, which is an apt analogy since he is one of the world's experts on natural soil use, but then he blew it.

He veered over into my field and started to talk about theology. He explained how there were three levels of Christian life: the conversion experience, the baptism with the Spirit, and then the third baptism, the baptism of fire or the baptism of suffering.

"No one is really a member of God's kingdom," he said, "until he's had the baptism with fire. You're not in God's kingdom until this experience happens to you."

All my theological bells started clanging. My ticker-tape verses began to go wild. "Except ye . . . become as little children, ye shall not enter into the kingdom of heaven" (Matt. 18:3, KJV). If a little child can make it, why can't I? Or Jesus' words to the poor, "Blessed are the poor in spirit, for theirs is the kingdom of heaven" (Matt. 5:3). If I am poor in spirit, why am I not a part of God's kingdom, whether I've had this "third experience" or not? "For the kingdom of God is not meat and drink, but righteousness and peace and joy in the Holy Ghost" (Rom. 14:17). If I have righteousness, peace, and joy, why am I not in the kingdom? Did not Paul show us that the world is only divided into two classes, those who are in Christ and those who are not?

Yet in the middle of my defensiveness I suddenly saw myself sitting across the room in the form of my friend. And I was reacting exactly the way my old associates had reacted—I was threatened by my friend's claim that he had discovered something new. I was angered that he had intimated I needed more. I felt left out, rejected, and I was inwardly angry, accusing him of pride and exclusiveness. As the roles reversed I realized, to my shame, what I had done to my friends in the past. I had unconsciously and unwittingly alienated them. I had wanted to help them, but I had hurt them. They heard so much "rightness" from me that they couldn't hear the witness I was trying to bear. How wrong I was. I began to pray, "Lord, I repent. Show me the depths of the artful arrogance that separates me from my evangelical and fundamentalist brothers. O Lord, you died to save all men. You love all of us who know and call upon your Name. Forgive me and make me a builder of unity."

I was not willing to say my new friend's theological reasoning was valid. In fact, I think his doctrine is haywire. But the Holy Spirit used his false doctrine to point out my false attitudes. Never again will I try to lord it over those who disagree.

4

What About Faith in the Logos?

Is it proper to pray for a sick person even though you do not have a direct word from God (*rhema*) to do so? Must the *rhema* from God arrive before you have permission to pray for the sick? Should you have some special word before you can pray with faith at all?

Absolutely not. Of course we pray for the sick when we have no special word from the Lord; many are healed in this way. On the other hand, it's not safe to depend upon our feelings as evidence God is healing.

One night, following the evening service at Tulsa Christian Fellowship, I felt a special anointing for healing. A lovely young lady came forward for prayer. She was legally blind and had been quite distressed in her Christian experience. When I reached out to touch her that night my hands were literally vibrating. The moment I touched her head she collapsed in the chair where she was sitting, slumping forward and almost falling out of the chair.

When she opened her eyes she could see. Her sight was not restored 100 percent, but there had been such a marked improvement she was overjoyed. She began to shout praises to the Lord.

The anointing seemed to remain; my hands were still vibrating. I began to move around the room praying for others who were sick. I said to myself, "Chuck, tonight the Lord is really present. You'd better move while the power is there!" As rapidly as I could, I prayed for several more. To my knowledge, no physical healing transpired for any of them. The feeling continued, but there was no virtue in that feeling whatsoever. I came away from the meeting having learned again it is the Lord who heals. Whatever our experiences may be, we simply act from obedience. When He heals, we praise Him. When He does not heal, we still give Him thanks. It is His to heal, ours to obey.

In fact, the majority of people are healed without the person who prays for them knowing whether healing is taking place or not. Many times they themselves are not sure what has happened and the healing takes place gradually and over a period of time.

Sometimes when we feel there's a real power going out from us, nothing apparently happens. At other times when we ourselves have felt absolutely nothing, there have been wonderful results.

It isn't wrong to pray for people simply on the basis of faith in God's Word. Jesus commands us to "heal the sick" (Matt. 10:8). Whether anyone is healed or not, we must, in obedience to Jesus, pray for the sick. It is part of the gospel. There is no escaping this conclusion. The real question is not, Why are not more healed? The real question is, Why don't we praise God more for the healings He does give? It isn't wrong to pray for people simply on the basis of God's Word. What is wrong is to tell people they are healed when there really is no word from God. I don't tell people they are healed simply because I have prayed. That is not faith; it is presumption. I don't say, "Throw away your glasses," when in fact the driver's license states they must wear glasses. I don't say, "Toss away your insulin," when I know them to be diabetics. I don't break crutches simply because I am a man of God. That is not bold faith. It is prideful presumption.

Before we proceed further with our study, a word of caution is in order. The distinction between *logos* and *rhema* does not hold true in every Bible passage. Throughout the Bible the differences in the ways these words are used varies greatly. Luke, at least in places, seems to reverse John's pattern of *logos* and *rhema*. Paul, curiously enough, uses only *logos* in Romans 3, 9, 13, 14 and 16 while Romans 10 uses only *rhema*. Not only are there differences among various authors in the way they use these two words (i.e., Luke and John), there are also differences between usages in the LXX (Septuagint) and the New Testament.

John consistently uses *logos* to exhibit the universal, the eternal. In the wonderful prologue to his Gospel, he speaks of Jesus in these terms. Jesus is the eternal, universal Word. If we studied only John, we would conclude that whenever an eternal, universal word was needed, *logos* would be used. But Peter does not follow John's lead. On at least one occasion, he uses *rhema* exactly the way John would have used *logos*. First Peter 1:25 tells us, "But the word of the Lord abides forever." Naturally, we should expect Peter to use *logos;* instead he uses *rhema*.

Since the Scriptures, therefore, do not teach a clear and unambiguous distinction between these two words, let us refer to the distinction between *logos* and *rhema* as a theological construct. A theological construct is a tool of analysis that enables us to see God's truth more clearly, without necessarily having complete scriptural endorsement. In other words, one could find support for both sides of a theological construct in Scripture. We use theological constructs most of the time without knowing it. For example, it is popular in most evangelical circles to refer to man as composed of body, soul and spirit; in other words, as a tripartite being. On the basis of this understanding, many evangelicals teach that there is a clear-cut distinction between soul and spirit. You have probably heard, as I have, long discourses on the difference between the soul and the spirit, how you can tell whether a song or a message is "soulish" or "spiritual," and how you can encourage the spiritual and eliminate the soulish. Exegetically, there are few Scriptures in the whole Bible that support this threefold distinction. First Thessalonians 5:23 and Hebrews 4:12 are the main support Scriptures.

The overwhelming evidence is that often soul and spirit are used interchangeably. However, many teachers find it useful to conceive of man in three parts, to distinguish between the soul and the spirit. Therefore, this is a theological construct, not a doctrine of the Church. It is in this way, then, that we use *logos* and *rhema*. It is simply a teaching tool that helps us to understand the difference between a general and a particular word of the Lord. Let us remember, then, that for our purposes *rhema* represents the "now" word of the Lord, the word that is quickened to me, the word that has become revelation, but let us not draw from that distinction that this is the way *rhema* is always used in the Bible. Like the distinction between soul and spirit, the distinction between *rhema* and *logos* cannot be used as a solid doctrinal distinctive, for the simple reason that Scriptures, except in John, often use *logos* and *rhema* interchangeably.

Did the Disciples Know the Difference?

Instinctively, the disciples knew the difference between a word that applied to all of them, and a word for a particular person. In Matthew 14:22-25, the disciples had an exciting experience, and began crossing the Sea of Galilee in a small boat. They had just finished a tremendous day of ministry. The day had ended with a grand finale—5,000 men, besides women and children, were miraculously fed. The warm glow of satisfaction that always attends God's special blessings kept them rowing hard through the stormy night. But they could make no progress at all.

Suddenly, out of nowhere, an apparition approached, walking on the water. They were terrified. They cried out, "It's a ghost!" But immediately the apparition spoke. The Master said, "Take heart, it is I; have no fear" (Matt. 14:27). What a glorious reassurance, but they weren't too confident even yet. There was a moment of unbelieving silence. Then Peter voiced it for all of them. "Lord, if that's really you, let me walk on the water too!'' Jesus spoke a single word, "Come." I imagine Peter thought, "Oh, no! Me and my big mouth." But he had no choice, the dye was cast. Crawling over the gunwale, he hit the water and began to run. To his surprise it held him up as he rushed toward Jesus. But the storm got to him. He took his eyes off Jesus and became the victim of his fear. He was desperate. "Lord, save me," he shouted. And Jesus did just that. When He got to the boat He gave Peter a little lecture on faith. "O man of little faith, why did you doubt?" (Matt. 14:31). If Peter had only a "little faith" and managed to run on water, imagine how the rest felt!

Point is, everybody in that boat knew that the command to come was for Peter alone. It was an invitation solely intended for him. I don't know of a single Christian theologian who has read this passage and said, "In the Greek (it always has to be in the Greek) this passage clearly teaches Peter was commanded to walk on water. Since Peter was a believer and we are believers, all believers can do the same. Burn the boats, boys, from now on we're walking on water!" Silly, isn't it? Yet I'm afraid that many of us go about burning boats when we would do better to "rightly divide the Word." We universalize a word intended for someone else.

A tragic example are Don and Kay, a young couple I knew in Tulsa. Don had been one of my seminary students, and had helped us loyally in a coffeehouse ministry I had initiated among blacks in North Tulsa in 1968. He was serious and conscientious in everything he attempted. He was also sensitive and compassionate. "An ideal young pastor," I thought. Several years after he graduated and moved, I accepted an invitation to address a conference in his city. On Sunday morning I was to speak in his church. When I met him, he appeared even more serious than I had remembered. Kay was more subdued too. I didn't think too much about it at the time.

Don's church was a classical Pentecostal church. The morning service moved smoothly enough, and there was a sweet spirit, but there was something missing. I had expected free worship and praise and had hoped to be blessed by some anointed, searching prophecies. In spite of my Presbyterian background, I had come to see that worship and praise were fully as important as the ministry of the Word, but nothing of the sort happened. At lunch he and his wife leaned forward to share. I shall never forget the forlorn, quiet sadness in his voice as he unfolded the tragic tale of how he had almost come to forsake the ministry.

A healing evangelist had taken a series of meetings in his church. Some people had been helped. This evangelist taught "confession is possession" without qualification. If you confessed your healing, possession would inevitably come. A positive confession always resulted in a positive possession. Newly baptized in the Spirit, a college professor who had suffered for years from diabetes listened with bated breath. He wanted to believe so badly. Finally, on Thursday night he screwed up his courage, walked down the aisle, and received prayer for his healing, knowing full well that this meant he would have to go off his insulin. The evangelist had made that abundantly clear. To take insulin amounted to a negative confession, a lack of faith. When you exercised faith, medicine was not necessary.

The professor was eager to hold on to his healing at any cost. He couldn't give up now, he had waited too long; he had staked too much on this opportunity. Word spread throughout the church. People rejoiced at the "healing," but the man grew weaker and weaker. His wife was frantic with fear. It didn't seem possible he could last until Sunday, but he did. Just barely.

Finally the evangelist got wind of the trouble, rushed into the stricken man's room, and immediately sensed the fearful agony of his wife. Leaving the husband for a moment, he turned to the wife and shouted, "You demon of fear! Come out of her. Come out in Jesus' Name!"

Then he whirled back to the dying man. "You're going to be all right," he said. "Just hold on to your healing. Everything is going to be just fine." As suddenly as he appeared, he was gone.

But everything was not "just fine." The tension built up in that small room until Don could stand it no more. He rushed to the phone. An ambulance screamed its way through the afternoon, and the man's life was barely saved. The doctor told Don, "One more hour and that man would most certainly have died."

Fortunately, the man lived, but Don was a chastened and troubled young man. Heartsick, confused and guilt-ridden, he almost left the ministry. What had gone wrong? Didn't God heal any more? Hadn't the evangelist preached the Word? Why wasn't the man healed? I couldn't answer his questions then, but I now know that part of the answer lies in knowing the difference between *logos*, God's general word of healing, and *rhema*, God's special word of healing for you.

Don's questions haunt me until this day. And I have to ask myself a few hard questions as well. Could someone hear me preach on the necessity of a positive confession, God's will and power to heal the sick, and do what the professor did? Could someone hear me teach the necessity of positive prayer and misunderstand? I often emphasize, "In praying for the sick, I never say, 'If it be thy will,' but I always pray positively, 'Lord, heal this man.' " Could someone take that to mean that healing is automatic? At any rate, it has taught me to be very careful what I say to people in need of healing unless I am sure that what I say is from God.

I am certain the evangelist had no intention of injuring anybody. But bad theology has a habit of being stiff and rigid. Sometimes it seems that preachers and theologians say, "My mind is made up. Don't confuse me with the facts. If the facts conflict with my theory, so much the worse for the facts." Granted, there is a vast difference between truth and facts, especially in spiritual areas. Facts are based on knowledge; truth on spiritual revelation and faith. Facts can be deceiving. Medical doctors often call certain diseases incurable or terminal. They base this on scientific fact. Truth, however, says "nothing is impossible with God." At the same time, to "confess" you don't have a broken leg when the bone is splintered and protruding through the skin is not truth—that is sheer foolishness, presumption. Therefore truth must also involve facts, not be limited by them or ignored by them. For that reason I teach my students: "If your theology conflicts with the facts, you'd better reexamine your theology."

Actually, if Christianity cannot exist as a miracle religion amidst the harsh realities of everyday life, and if it cannot survive in this particular arena of history, the twentieth century, it doesn't deserve to endure. If Jesus did not actually heal the halt, lame and blind, then let's look somewhere else for our answers. If Christ did not physically rise from the dead, then Paul is right, our faith would be vain. Bad theology is a cruel taskmaster, and he flogs his children with tragic consequences. He cripples those who receive him, just as surely as the torture cages of Vietnam did.

Not too long ago I was talking to a man whose mother had been badly wounded by some words of bad theology. A preacher laid five words on her that crippled her and turned her into a guilt-ridden, miserable, joyless old woman long before her time. The words that made her surrender her joy for bitterness were these: "You are living in adultery." It is even more tragic when one considers that biblically these words were not justified.

Some time ago a young friend of mine had been sitting in the "hot chair" asking for healing. Suddenly he was aware of another sinister presence. The demon began to speak through his voice. It was an eerie experience. The people, in real consternation, prayed. Finally the spirit left. My friend was healed and grateful, but their theology did not permit him to have a demon, so they told him that what had obviously happened did not occur. Now my friend is ostracized from the group, all because their theology taught that no Christian could be under bondage to a demon spirit. Bad theology is indeed a cruel taskmaster.

For the past twenty years, as I have studied theology, I am more and more convinced that nothing is more rigid or more opposed to the Holy Spirit's blessed moving in our age than bad theology. That is why many theologians don't care much for the book of Acts. The Holy Spirit keeps upsetting their theological applecart. Just when they have everything figured out, the Holy Spirit does things in a different way. Bad theology says that miracles cannot occur in our century. Bad theology says no Christian can be tortured by a demon. Bad theology says only lack of faith prevents healing.

In fact, bad theology is like the cruel giant Procrustes—the highwayman from Attica. When visitors arrived at his castle, he stretched them out on a carefully prepared iron bed. If they were too long, he cut off their legs. If they were too short, he stretched them to fit. That is what bad theology does. If it doesn't fit the facts, cut off the facts. If the facts are contrary to the Bible, bad theology says, "That's easy enough, just stretch the facts."

Others believe all theology is unnecessary. Some say, "I don't have any theology; I just believe in Jesus." They may not know it, but "just believing in Jesus" is already a pretty profound theological statement. If you haven't got a good theology, it is pretty likely you will have a bad one.

God gave us minds. We have an obligation to use them. Jesus told the curious lawyer that the greatest commandment reads: "You shall love the Lord your God with all your heart, and with all your soul, and with all your mind. This is the great and first commandment" (Matt. 22:37-38). We must learn to love God with our minds as well as our hearts.

Spirit-filled people often downgrade intellectual endeavor. This is understandable, because it is certainly true that the intellect is no substitute for the spirit, but neither was the spirit meant to substitute for the rightful domain of the mind. Both were meant to function in their proper spheres. Each without the other is incomplete. Isn't this why the apostle Paul instructs the exuberant Corinthians in the midst of their excitement over the gifts, "My brothers, don't be like excitable children but use your intelligence! By all means be innocent as babes as far as evil is concerned, but where your minds are concerned be full-grown men" (1 Cor. 14:20, Phillips).

True enough, simplicity is an attribute of deity, but there is such a thing as oversimplifying matters, ending in half-truths, disappointments and frustrated hopes. Simplicity can be of two kinds: a premature kind of simplicity that reduces everything to a formula and thereby fails to treat all the evidences, limiting itself to what it can explain; or the simplicity that is godlike because it has faced all the complexities of contradictory evidences and still affirms the simplicity of faith. I suspect the difference lies in attitude; in a simplistic simplicity, arrogance is the besetting sin because you do, after all, have the answers. In the other, humility is the guiding characteristic because there is so much that we do not know. We must learn to embrace the simplicity that has come through complexity and shun the simplicity that has not fully addressed the question. Pascal spoke of two kinds of ignorance: the ignorance that has come through the knowledge we have and knows we know nothing, and the ignorance that is simply ignorance. We seem to be so gimmick-prone. One rebukes the enemy, bad financial situations end, and the money flows in. One praises God and even his personal sins are overlooked. One claims his healing and it automatically comes. One gets baptized in the Spirit and this guarantees instant health, wealth, and fame. All problems dissolve if only you can get the right formula working.

Let's face it squarely. We are always confronted by problems and will never be finally delivered from difficulties in this present life. Even Paul says, "Wretched man that I am! Who will deliver me from this body of death?" (Rom. 7:24). As long as we live we are never out of trouble, for we soon discover that conflict is the name of the game. That is why Paul's favorite picture of the soldier is so apt. There may be a lull in the battle, but there's never a cessation of hostilities. There is no simple solution that will solve all our problems. We may as well face the harsh fact that the war is never over, and our struggles will not cease until we reach the other side. To the extent that Hegel perceived life to be a struggle between forces and counter-forces, a contest of wills, a striving to be in the midst of becoming, he was an astute analyst of the human scenario.

A theology of healing, thus, has a very difficult task. It must walk a hairline. On the one hand it must avoid the Scylla of presumption, and on the other hand it must avoid the Charybdis of unbelief. If we have been too zealous for faith that is not always according to knowledge and is sometimes presumptuous, better we should curb the excess than deal with those who don't believe enough to venture out in faith at all. After all, it's easier to steer a rolling stone than to budge a lodged boulder! If we must err, let us err on the side of a bold, positive faith.

True faith always seems to face the problem of Luther's drunken peasant. He mounts his horse but falls off first one side, then the other. Somehow there has to be a balance here between presumption and unbelief. We must look to God to give us a balanced theology of healing that is positive, expectant, and yet somehow avoids falling into presumption.

5

Some of the Nitty-Gritty Questions of Healing and Death

We need to take a long hard look at the doctrine of healing. Webster defines health as being whole or hale and sound in body, mind, or soul, especially freedom from physical disease or pain. That's a good secular definition, but it omits the most important part—health for the spirit. When the spirit is sick, the body and the mind also suffer. It is not possible to be sick in your spirit and be a whole man. It is the hardest kind of healing to obtain because the sickness of the spirit is what the Bible calls sin. Sin is the hardest thing of all to cure. I used to wonder if it was a cop-out when people said, "Spiritual healing is the main consideration of a healing prayer." When I first heard the teaching, "Remember that the real healing is spiritual," I thought, "What a lovely loophole! If this poor man gets no help, they can always say, 'But the spiritual healing is the main thing.' If I were really in pain that would be poor comfort indeed."

Over the years I've come to see the wisdom of these words. I am convinced that by far the hardest healing to obtain is genuine healing for the spirit. In fact, I know of many physical healings that occur through natural or psychological processes, but I've never known a single spiritually sick individual to be healed except by the supernatural divine work of God. After all, sin is the only ultimately fatal disease. I have learned to ask God for insight into the spirits of the physically ill, because when they are spiritually well they are virtually unconquerable, even by death. Physical sickness is not life's worst illness.

Since we've heard so much about God's will for our physical healing, it's hard to accept the fact that a person may be perfectly healthy in his spirit and yet be wasting away to death in his body. Even Paul speaks of the paradox of dying in order to live. "As unknown, and yet well known; as dying, and behold we live; as punished and yet not killed . . ." (2 Cor. 6·9). We must accept the fact that there is a time when Jesus says to His saints, "It's time to come home!"

I recall the painful death of my neighbor Nancy. She had a good, solid church background in a Bible-teaching church where she had truly met the Lord. Both she and her husband had gotten busy in a good many civic enterprises, until tragedy struck. Cancer brought Nancy down. She tried everything: the best that science could offer, as well as the more exotic cures such as laetrile. Nothing worked. She steadily grew worse.

During her last days I visited her a number of times. I could feel her hesitating as she and I conversed about the inevitable. One day she spoke these electrifying words:

"Chuck, I simply don't want to live." I looked down at her wasted ninety-seven-pound body. She was simply skin and bones. Her face was tired with long lines of weariness etched by pain. A hundred sleepless nights and a hundred weary days. What would you have said?

She went on. "I suppose it's wrong to feel this way, but I am simply too tired to go on. I've made all my plans. Now I want to die." I sat silently listening, trying to hear her hurt and enter into her weariness. I know from the way she hesitated that she expected a lecture from me on the necessity of trying hard to live. I know that she was anticipating the time-honored clichés expected of a clergyman: "Keep up the fight! Don't give up the ship. Jesus wants to heal you." And I guess I half expected myself to say something of the sort as well, but no words came. I simply sat silent and nodded. I know she took courage from my silence because she reopened the subject again. Once again I had nothing to say.

I will never forget the last time I visited her. It was on a Sunday afternoon right after church and I slipped over to the hospital to see how she was doing. There she tossed restlessly back and forth. Her courageous, patient husband was standing by her side, holding her hand. She held on as tightly as she could, never taking her eyes from him as though he were her life raft in a very stormy sea, and as her restless body continued to twist and turn, gasping for breath, clinging to John, he never so much as lifted his eyes to greet me. Their eyes seemed riveted together. I wondered how he stood so long, hardly twitching a muscle.

I felt like an awkward intruder, like some bungling

bumpkin who had unwittingly stumbled onto a scene meant for no other human eyes; and I shifted from foot to foot. I cleared my throat and wondered if there were some way I could gracefully leave. Seldom have I felt so inadequate. I wanted to bolt and run but I knew that dying people often hear and understand long after we think they are gone. How could I leave gracefully? I determined to stay.

John spoke, "Chuck's here." A little whimper of pain, a small acknowledgment of humiliation that I should see her so distressed and agitated, that was all. But I knew I had some words from the Lord for her. "Nancy," I said, "I want to pray with you." I held her paper-thin wrist and began to beseech the Father. As I prayed I felt a strange anointing of the Spirit and knew God was at work. "Lord, I thank you that though we walk through the valley of the shadow of death, you are with us. Though we are in pain, you are there. Though our lives slip away, you stand beside us because you said you would. You promised never to leave us nor to forsake us. O Lord, we thank you that in the darkest night you hold us tightly and we thank you for Jesus who carries us carefully through the valley of the shadow into His bosom. In Jesus' Name, amen."

I left. The next morning as I was praying a thought came to me. "Relinquish Nancy. Send her on her way."

I have known of cases where Christians unwittingly delay the departure of some loved one by well-intentioned prayers that hold them here. Often we become so intent upon getting people healed we fail to discern or ask for the will of God in a given situation. We concentrate so hard on the healing that we forget the Healer. Particularly is this true when a young person is involved. Somehow we all feel that the young simply should not die. It never occurs to us to relinquish them into the hand of the Lord.

I recalled Tom, a fine minister friend of mine, who became deeply, emotionally involved in the health of a pathetic little twelve-year-old girl who simply could not survive medically. She had wasted away to an infant's size. I remember looking down at the skeleton-like form, where she spoke with a voice so weak that it kept fading in and out as her strength came and went. I wondered if it really was a kindness to keep her here. But Tom was so intent, so insistent on her healing, that we all joined him. Our church prayed for a miracle healing, as did the prayer groups. But one day Tom came to a higher understanding and he prayed the prayer of relinquishment. He relinquished this dear child to the arms of Jesus. That same day she died.

If it is possible for people to die before their appointed time, as Paul certainly seems to teach (1 Cor. 11:29-30), is it not also possible for the powerful prayers of the saints to keep people alive beyond their intended time?

At any rate, I felt moved to pray the prayer of relinquishment for Nancy. I prayed, "Lord Jesus, I relinquish Nancy into your loving care. I know you love her far more than I ever could. I give her back to you, loving Lord Jesus. She is yours." That was at 7:00 A.M. At 8:30 A.M. she died.

Her funeral was a triumphant affair. Nancy had received her final coronation. She was safe with Jesus, happier, more secure than she had ever been. Then I thought about her illness and how her spirit grew clearer, stronger, and more triumphant each day on earth. She knew Jesus at the time of her death better than she had ever known Him in life. As her poor body wasted away, she came to a deeper, purer knowledge of the Lord. Not always do physical and spiritual well-being go hand in hand.

Another question concerning death intrigued me. How far should we go to preserve life? Does God always demand heroic means to maintain life that is no longer meaningful? Jim was a neighbor who taught me far more than he will ever know. My daughter Melissa played often with his lovely daughter of the same age. Then they moved away to another section of town and I never had a chance to witness to Jim. I briefly regretted this. He was a good businessman, known for his fairness to his employees, but his busy life seemed to crowd God out. One day when I went to pick Melissa up at his house, God gave me an unexpected opportunity. At the same time I was jolted.

Jim said, "Chuck, have you got a moment?"

"Of course."

"The doctor just told me I have at most two years to live. I am dying of A.L.S. (Lou Gehrig's disease)."

I asked, "Are you sure?"

"Yes, I'm sure. There are no known cures for A.L.S. It is 100 percent fatal."

After the initial shock I sat down and chatted with Jim for a while. "Are you quite certain, Jim, that you are ready to go to your Maker?" I asked.

"No, I'm not really sure, Chuck," he responded. That night I went through a little salvation booklet, "How to Have a Happy Forever," that I had written and Don Woods had illustrated with his well-known little character,

"Gusty." Jim was not ready to receive Christ that night, but on the second visit he made a beautiful, firm decision for Christ, from which he never wavered over the long, dreary months of his illness.

I explained to Jim how Jesus willed our healing and that just as He had performed many wonderful miracles while on earth when He was here, He was performing the same miracles today. "Jesus Christ is the same yesterday and to day and for ever" (Heb. 13:8). But I was also careful not to promise Jim a miraculous cure. The elders and pastors of our church anointed him with oil according to James 5:14.

I visited Jim often because I knew how vital follow-up was for a new Christian. But Jim more often inspired me than I him. He read his Bible regularly and prayed for strength to help others. He began visiting other A.L.S. victims and did everything in his power to bring strength and comfort to them.

His speech grew increasingly slurred. Soon it was difficult to understand him, finally impossible. Then we communicated by writing. It was hard on him and me.

One day Jim scribbled a note to me that the last months of his life had been the happiest he'd ever known. I was overjoyed. His witness among his friends was outstanding. All his friends commented on the change in his life, and his continued attempts to help others became well known.

At last he could survive no longer without heroic measures. This included intravenous feeding and around-the-clock nursing care. He was hooked up to all the machines and gadgets that can keep a man alive today, but it really never was his desire to sustain life by machines.

He indicated to Bill, the senior pastor and my beloved co-laborer at Tulsa Christian Fellowship, that he really wanted to go home. Bill asked him if he meant his own home in South Tulsa, but he pointed upwards. I am thinking of Paul's burning wish, "I am hard pressed between the two. My desire is to depart and be with Christ, for that is far better" (Phil. 1:23). I suppose some well-meaning preacher today would have rushed up to the apostle and said, "Now, Paul, that's all wrong! You're supposed to live for the here and now. You shouldn't even think about such things, never mind write such a thing for Holy Scripture. Whatever can you be about?"

But Jim wanted to go home. Medical science didn't permit this. Month after month his agony was prolonged. His lungs had to be constantly drained or he would have drowned in his own body fluids. It was a painful, excruciating process that had to take place every half-hour. He had to be watched constantly, because on more than one occasion he had tried to pull out the cluttered paraphernalia that prolonged his life. I could hardly blame him for the attempts he made. It was painful to watch him waste away to a skeleton, kept alive only by means of medical marvels. Had science in its kindness now become cruel? In the endeavor to save life, does God insist that we perpetuate life long after it serves no useful purpose and only prolongs the pain? What an enormous amount of money is squandered on people who doctors know cannot survive. For the Christian, death is not the end, but the beginning. At last Jim succumbed. I was relieved, though sorry, to see my friend go. Jim had his wish; he had gone home

There seems something unseemly to me about a system that keeps people alive as vegetables long after they have lost their dignity and worthwhileness as human beings. Jesus never died—he simply dismissed His spirit (Matt. 27:50). In classical Greek the word used is "to discharge," "to send forth," "to let go." In the Greek New Testament when it is used with a person it means "to let go," "to send away." Jesus was in full command of His faculties at the time of His death. He died with dignity as befitted the Son of God. Does He not give us the example to follow in death as in life? I don't really know all the answers or how I will feel in the future, but at the present time I am ready to reject all heroic means to preserve life when death is imminent. Despite the opinion that seems to prevail widely in many charismatic circles that life ought to go on endlessly and effortlessly, I am stuck with Paul. I still desire to be with Christ "which is far better." Yes, there are worse things than death. Certainly living as a vegetable falls into that category for the Christian.

A spirit in bondage is extremely difficult to cure—in fact, impossible outside of that wonderful, mysterious expression of God's love to us, the grace of God. For example, as I was originally preparing this study a stricken mother called. Her son was facing ten years in the state prison and after that five more years at a federal penitentiary. He looked awful and could not sleep. He was frightened, drawn and anxious. He had recurring dreams of murder and they were particularly alarming to him. When he was with his mother he explained, "You see, mother, I dream of killing people; but the thing that frightens me most is that in the last year or two all of my dreams have come true.''

Imprisoned men kill for the most trivial reasons. Someone steals a man's milk and he is killed, or someone refuses a man his proper amount of food and he kills. Life is cheap in prison and young men resort to great violence with the slightest provocation.

But this young man's real problem was neither the prison nor his dreams. His real problem grew out of his relationship with his father. From the time he was a baby his father seemed to be jealous of the time his mother gave to him. The mother was sure that the father had never fully forgiven the boy for the time he had taken or the trouble he had been. Yes, he was a Christian, but this sickness of the spirit, this inability to forgive a son who went astray, may be finally a factor in somebody's unnecessary murder. That son can never be fully free until the father sets him free by totally and utterly forgiving him. To gain health here is very difficult. The sicknesses of the spirit can only be dealt with through the supernatural work of Christ.

Or take the young lady in our fellowship who was trying in vain to receive the baptism of the Spirit. She had tried everything, but her freedom in a heavenly language simply did not come. She struggled and struggled. She had obeyed all the instructions. What could possibly be wrong? A thought knifed her heart. *You must forgive your father.* "O Lord, you don't know what you're asking." Forgive her father? Impossible. Her thoughts stole back to that tragic day when she was alone with him. He began to kiss and fondle her. She was horrified and yet strangely fascinated. Then came the awful deed that scarred her childhood memories and blocked her spiritual freedom. Nor had he escaped unscathed. The oppressive guilt, the pressures of life, drove him to a series of irrational acts that resulted in his incarceration in a mental institution where he sat day after day, dull, unresponsive and despondent. She struggled with the thought that had come to her by the Spirit's gentle prodding. How could she forgive him? But God's grace took over, and before she knew it, she whispered, "Oh, Lord, I forgive my father." Immediately there came a release in the Spirit she had never known before, a new joy and a new freedom exhilarated her. Her heavenly language flowed. She was thrilled with the experience which lifted her to a level of forgiveness she had never known. This occurred on a Wednesday.

On Friday her sister called. She said, "Guess what! I visited dad on Wednesday. He seemed to be so much more free and cheerful than I have seen him for a long time." How good God is! What power there is in forgiveness! Here the father, although situated some distance from his daughter, was really set free by her forgiving spirit and responded to the release he himself unconsciously felt.

Is Healing in the Atonement?

One of the most crucial questions concerning healing is this: Is healing in the Atonement? If it is, can we count on God's healing power today? But further, if we meet all the conditions, why are not all who are prayed for healed? The Scriptures seem clear. Isaiah 53:4 literally says, "Surely our sicknesses He himself bore and our pains He himself carried. Yet we ourselves esteemed Him stricken, smitten of God and afflicted." There is little question but that physical healing is placed under the sign of the cross. It is an integral part of the redemption process. As Leslie Weatherhead says, "It was God's ideal purpose for every man to enjoy perfect health of body, soul, and spirit." That is certainly true to the whole tenor of the New Testament.

Furthermore, it is very clear that healing and the Atonement are bound together. If healing is not in this passage, neither can we count on anything else. Andrew Murray points out that healing is strongly taught in this passage. Delitzsch assures us that in this verse where it speaks of both salvation and healing (Isa. 53:4) the "mediatorial sense remains the same."[5] As Christ took our sins upon Him and acted as mediator between us and the Father, so He took our sicknesses upon Him in a substitionary way. This does not mean merely a symbol, but *in our stead* and *in our place*, and He not only took them away, *but bore them for us*.

Why Are Not All Healed?

Surely it is one of the glories of the present age that we understand anew that Jesus still stands ready, able, and eager to heal! It is abundantly clear from an exegesis of Isaiah 53 that healing is in the Atonement and yet it doesn't seem to work automatically. Why not? Why are not all healed who exercise faith?

I think part of the answer lies in dispensational truth. I am not talking now about a system of fundamentalism called dispensationalism, but I am speaking of a dispensational understanding which recognizes that God reveals His truths and blessings to mankind in time sequences. Jesus pointed out that the age of grace so far superseded the age of law that even John the Baptist, of whom Jesus said, "There has risen no one greater," was less than the least in the kingdom of God (Matt. 11:11). Paul speaks of the "dispensation of the fulness of times" (Eph. 1:10, KJV) when all things will be united in Christ. Now in this age of grace we can say freely to all men, "Repent, believe, and you will be saved." In twenty-seven years of ministry I have never known or met an exception. I have known people who could not believe. I have met people who would not repent, but I have never met anyone, anyplace, anywhere in the world who repented, believed, and was not saved It is a universal maxim, whenever a man anywhere truly repents and believes in Jesus, he is saved. Not only is this truth found in Scripture, but it's true to our experience. All who repent, believe, and are baptized (although the interpretation of this latter phrase is too complex to be discussed at this time) are saved. Now think with me for a moment. Can we say with equal force and inner assurance reinforced by experience, "Repent, believe, and you will be healed"? Consider that believing Christian you know who was never healed. All of us are acquainted with some wonderful saints of God who've walked with Him for years and yet have not received their healing. Are you willing to say, "They had no faith. They would not confess their healing. If they had, they would all have been healed"?

When I worked with Miss Kathryn Kuhlman it was a curious but incontestable fact that many of her most ardent admirers, who prayed for her daily and were great believing Christians, simply were never healed. Yet there were a number of old rascally roustabouts who hadn't been inside a church for fifty years and had come to scoff—utterly without faith—who were suddenly and miraculously touched by the grace and mercy of God. This used to cause me excruciating pain. "Lord, did you see that? Did you see that old boozer get healed just now?" Sometimes I could hardly stand it. It seemed so unfair, especially in the light that many of the praying, severely crippled saints, who attended every single meeting, were never healed. It's a total mystery. I have no explanation.

I remember being in one of Kathryn's great meetings. A backslidden Jewish believer came bounding down the aisle.

"What was your problem, sir?" I inquired.

"I was so racked with pain from arthritis that I could hardly move," he said. "I didn't want to come here. I wanted to go to the races. My wife dragged me here instead. I was sitting back there crying because of the pain, wishing I were somewhere else, when suddenly I was healed." His whole countenance was beaming.

It was obvious that he had been healed. He was bouncing around the auditorium like a three-year-old, renewed in body and soul, praising God for His great mercy. Kathryn's favorite song, "He Touched Me," had come true for him. Yet, sitting in front of him was a godly, praying, fasting, believing sister with cancer, who left the meeting as unhealed as when she arrived.

Healing is related to the mystery of the kingdom of God. It has to do with the divine mysteries of God's own dispensation. What we see now is the kingdom not yet fully restored, not yet fully come. Here we are like little children, surrounded by divine mystery, grateful for God's present provision of miracles and healings, which are like lightning flashes of sovereign love, illuminating our gloom and despair over the ravages of friends with incurable diseases—yet not satisfied with what we see. We are utterly bewildered by why God heals some and not others. Obviously God isn't as discriminatory as we are! As Weatherhead points out, what is done for man is not done by his faith but by Christ through His faith. He points out that faith is the psychological frame of mind in which God can get near enough to man in order to do His work. Since healing then is in the Atonement and God wills total health for His children, why are not all healed? I don't know. I simply don't know. I do know one thing, however: there's a mystery here we will never fully understand. We box God in with our syllogisms and God refuses to dance to our tune. If anything has become apparent to me in the ministry of healing it is that it offers a golden opportunity for any minister to proclaim the "Godness" of God. I rest easy in the sovereignty of a God whose "ways are not my ways; whose thoughts are not my thoughts," and who works in wondrous ways His mysteries to perform. God simply will not bow to our little syllogisms. Here is one favorite thesis in charismatic circles.

Major premise: Healing is in the Atonement.

Minor premise: Faith is the key to healing.

Conclusion: Therefore, those who are prayed for in faith will be healed.

Right? Not always. It just isn't that simple. There is always an X factor in healing, an unknown quantity that

God does not choose to reveal. Healing is a divine mystery and humility is our best approach to unraveling the answers. Otherwise, if we knew all the answers it would no longer be a mystery. We would be as gods and have no need for a faith dependency.

At one time recently we had in our area a woman who claimed a healing as remarkable as any that graced the pages of the New Testament. She had been in the last stage of terminal brain cancer and had become so ill she wasn't even able to move. She could only be carried on a stretcher. Somehow she decided to risk her life in attending one of the great healing services of Kathryn Kuhlman. She had been completely helpless for over a year, utterly incapable of performing even the simplest functions of life, lying there waiting to die. Somehow she was able to survive the crowds and the heat. As the miracle service progressed she suddenly felt great waves of healing warmth engulf her body. Miss Kuhlman was aware of the miracle taking place. When she received her usual word of knowledge, she singled her out from among the crowd. One of Miss Kuhlman's trusted lieutenants came to the woman's side and successfully got her on her feet. She staggered down the aisle, but a great soaring emotion grasped her heart with sheer elation, ''I can walk! I can walk!''

She felt utterly cleansed, totally healed by God's great miracle power, but that was only the beginning of God's gracious miracle work in her life. That very next week while standing in the shower she felt something. She was incredulous over what was taking place! To her utter unbelief, two brand-new breasts appeared in place of the double mastectomy she had had a few years before.

It was a fantastic story! I listened intently and tried to perceive her spirit. Her knowledge of medical terminology was impressive. She seemed honestly intent on honoring the Lord. Humble and open, her only concern appeared to be to give God the glory. A few weeks passed by. The news of her miraculous healing spread like wildfire. A young friend of mine was asked to handle her bookings, because she had so many invitations to speak. All over the area meetings in which she was the featured speaker appeared as if by magic.

Unfortunately her story was untrue. The hospitals that had supposedly served her had none of her records. The doctors named had never seen her or treated her. Copies and signatures of medical records she had showed had evidently been forged. The doctors involved denied ever seeing or signing the records. It was a hard blow for my young friend, John, who had worked night and day with local pastors all over the area, booking her and her remarkable story. But the biggest shock was still in store for him as he attempted to make things right with the local pastors.

"It's a hoax," he said. "I'm sorry I ever booked her in your church. Her stories have proved to be contradictory and false. When we checked her records, it was apparent she had never had cancer of the brain. Her breasts were never removed. The whole story is untrue."

To his complete surprise some of the pastors responded defensively to his revelations. One of them was downright indignant. "You're just trying to discredit her! It's only your word against hers. I've got her booked and that's that!

I've advertised and she's going to speak!"

It's almost impossible to dislodge someone from a cherished belief. The power of the human mind to deceive itself seems infinite. When people want to believe badly enough, it's practically impossible to dissuade them.

From Galileo on, the Church has often been the last place where ideas change. For better or worse, the Church has almost always been associated with the most conservative and sometimes reactionary ideas in politics and society. Throughout its long history the Church has seldom identified with the common people, the shirtless ones, the needy. It has most often appeared on the side of the rich and the vested interests. I have often wondered if this is because the Church has adopted an unconscious theological stance: "The poor are poor because they deserve to be poor."

When Jesus was here He proved to be the greatest and most radical revolutionary of them all. In fact, His revolution was the hardest and most difficult to come by because He called for a revolution of the heart, a radical change in the way men thought, worked, and believed. He taught that the kingdom of God was a present reality to those who could exercise faith. He was the only true revolutionary, because He worked for the only kingdom that ultimately counts, the kingdom where the beatitudes reign.

What Was Paul's "Thorn in the Flesh"?

There is little question but that healing is one of the chief signs of the coming of the kingdom of God. In Isaiah 61:1-3 it is clearly a kingdom sign that the Messiah would bring "good tidings to the afflicted; he has sent me to bind up the brokenhearted, to proclaim liberty to the captives, and the opening of the prison to those who are bound; to proclaim the year of the Lord's favor. . . ." Jesus certainly understood this passage as the signal that the kingdom had come. In Luke 4:16-21 Jesus entered Nazareth, His hometown, and went into the synagogue where He began to read from the Isaiah passage. His interpretation of the passage was astounding. He said, "Today this scripture has been fulfilled." Whatever else the crowd may have thought they could not help concluding that somehow the *new age* had come and Jesus was introducing himself as the *special agent* of its fulfillment. No wonder they approved! Nothing would have pleased them more than a messianic king who could deliver them from the power of Rome.

In healing, the early Church, too, always saw God's gracious fulfillment of the promised King and His kingdom. Beginning with Jesus' arguments in behalf of His messiahship addressed to the doubting disciples of John (Luke 7:20-23) and continuing through the chronicles of the early Church where the Church leaders called on God to heal as accrediting proofs of the Word they preached (Acts 4:27-30), healing was a sign of the kingdom. Paul's understanding is the same as that of the early Church. In fact, as one of the evidences of a true apostle, Paul enumerates the "signs and wonders and mighty works" (2 Cor. 12:12). Why then was Paul not more disturbed that he had to leave his companion, Trophimus, sick at Miletus (2 Tim. 4:20)? No apostle or New Testament writer ever said, "Though Aristarchus repented and believed, he was never saved." The New Testament writers clearly spoke in unison, "All who repent and believe are saved." But they never said, "All who repent and believe are healed."

In fact, their own experience was to the contrary. Not only was Trophimus left sick, but Paul enjoins Timothy to take a little wine for his stomach's sake (1 Tim. 5:23). Furthermore, there remains before us the difficult problem of Paul's thorn in the flesh. What was it? How did it operate? Why did it come?

The difficult passage reads: "And to keep me from being too elated by the abundance of revelations, a thorn was given me in the flesh, a messenger of Satan, to harass me, to keep me from being too elated. Three times I besought the Lord about this, that it should leave me, but he said to me, 'My grace is sufficient for you, for my power is made perfect in weakness.' I will all the more gladly boast of my weaknesses, that the power of Christ may rest upon me" (2 Cor. 12:7-9). In the New English Bible Paul says, "And so, to keep me from being unduly elated by the magnificence of such revelations, I was given a sharp pain in my body which came as Satan's messenger to bruise me; this was to save me from being unduly elated."

The essence of what Paul is saying is clear. In order that he may not be overly exalted, there was given to him a thorn in the flesh.[6] Calvin translates this as "goad"[7] instead of "thorn." But the word is *skolops*, an old word usually translated "splinter" or "thorn." In classical Greek it means "a stake," but that is not the sense in which it is used here. Most interpreters understand this to be a physical malady.[8] All sorts of physical problems have been suggested, including malaria, eye trouble, epilepsy, insomnia, migraine headaches, and even sensual temptation. There is no necessity to understand the stress as a physical malady. The text simply refers to a messenger of Satan. The word for messenger is the same word that is used for angel, *angelos*. It is used of persons. It therefore suggests a personal spirit sent from Satan with the specific purpose of harassing the apostle. The word used for harass is *kolaphizo*, which literally means ''to buffet, to slap in the face.''

So far the text is clear, it is not just any sickness; in fact, it may not be a physical malady at all, but it is a direct frontal attack by a demonic force assigned to hamper and harass Paul in his gospel work. This creature buffets him and treats him with indignity. Calvin writes: ''Accordingly, if anyone has had his face made black and blue, he does not from a feeling of shame venture to expose himself openly in the view of men.''[9]

The purpose of the buffeting, then, is to keep Paul humble. This helps him to avoid what Augustine calls ''the poison of pride.'' Some commentators see this affliction as attacking him in the flesh, the body. Calvin takes exception to this and views the flesh here to denote ''not the body, but that part of the soul which has not yet been regenerated.''[10] Most modern scholars prefer to think of this as a physical disorder, although as mentioned before, the Greek does not demand this interpretation. In my opinion, they opt for this solution because they do not fully understand the supernaturalist view of Paul. Paul knew well enough the distinction between physical sickness and a satanic attack, and to be true to the text we cannot understand this in a symbolic or hyperbolical sense. Paul literally underwent humiliating encounters with a foreign hostile entity that proved so personally difficult for him that he asked the Lord to remove it on at least three different occasions. Some commentators take this to mean earnest and repeated prayer, while others understand this in a literal sense, that is, three actual times Paul made it a specific matter of prayer.

Barrett opts for a speech impediment. This, he believes, would account for Paul's sometimes bad first impression and the fact that he was judged "poor in presence and speech but impressive in his letters" (2 Cor. 10:1, 9, 10, 11; 11.6).[11]

Is there any servant of the Lord who has not been troubled by some thorn in the flesh, visible or private, that often pursues him at the time of his greatest spiritual triumphs? I have often reflected on the fact that after an occasion when the Lord has used me in a particularly fruitful ministry, a "fly in the ointment" inevitably appears. I get a critical letter from a friend, I face a major family crisis, or someone wants to turn off my electricity In a general way, then, every servant of the Lord is troubled by a thorn in the flesh, but I do not feel that this rather ambiguous and vague explanation reflects a true understanding of Paul's specific trouble.

The view of Chrysostum has been recently gaining credence among a number of conservative scholars as the most likely explanation Chrysostum rejects out of hand the idea of a physical malady and understands the term "Satan" in the general Hebrew sense of "adversary."

Thus he understands Paul's adversaries, such as Alexander the coppersmith, Hymeneas and Philetus, as the messengers of Satan who harass him. Certainly it is true that Paul was harassed on every side by jealous Jews, false apostles, and backslidden Christians. But when we understand Paul's world, where the supernatural was part and parcel of everyone's daily experience, this explanation will not suffice.

In my opinion, the clearest and most simple explanation is the one Paul himself gives: There was a personal demonic entity assigned to him who from time to time harassed him in such a way that Paul was able to discern and identify the source of his problem as a messenger of Satan. And this agent was permitted to hinder him in some unknown but humiliating way.

Over the years when about to embark on some particularly significant ministry, I have observed the same sort of problem, although in no way do I perceive this to be of the same intensity or duration as that which afflicted the great apostle. As the time for the ministry approaches, my mind clouds up, my stomach is tortured by sharp, recognizable pains, I am afflicted by nausea and I am almost overwhelmed by a great unnatural weariness with waves of utter inadequacy and near panic. The temptation is always the same: "Don't go, give up. You're too sick to minister! You've nothing to say anyway. Call them while you're still alive!"

Some may argue, "Chuck, you're just feeling the usual nervousness a speaker feels." But I reject this because the type of activity I have just described is much more intense than ordinary malaise, and I feel in my spirit that I am literally battling against demonic oppression. In a sense it cannot be called a physical disease, but in another sense it does cause a temporary physical disorder and great mental distress. It definitely comes from the outside like a cloud of darkness and it often leaves as quickly as it comes. There is not the ordinary recovery span one expects when he recovers from, say, the flu. This harassment retreats at the name of Jesus and is kept at bay by verbally praising the Lord, but often does not subside until after the first meeting is over. If I were to try to identify it, I would be comfortable with the same terminology Paul uses: a messenger of Satan. Resisting the enemy in the Name of Jesus almost always proves effective, at least in helping me through the first meeting, and after the meetings are over and I look back in retrospect, there's almost always some major victory or unusual manifestation of God's power that explains the intensity of the demonic assault. I believe many ministers of the gospel could attest to the same facts.

When I started to summarize my findings, I reviewed some interesting facts. First, healing is always a sign of the Messiah and His kingdom. The kingdom message proclaims the universal gospel that offers salvation and healing to all who repent and believe. But apparently all who are saved are not necessarily healed. This poses a problem theologically because the same passage in Isaiah 53:3-5 that teaches the substitutionary atonement of our Lord also teaches that He will bear our sicknesses and diseases. It is difficult, for example, to conceive of Luke's great skill as a physician being a matter of indifference in his choice as the traveling companion of the apostle Paul, who quite probably needed Luke's medical administrations from time to time. At any rate, Paul does not seem unduly troubled by Trophimus' illness, Timothy's stomach weakness, or his own buffetings by Satan—which undoubtedly involved physical discomfort. Instead, he went right on preaching the gospel in the midst of his afflictions to everyone everywhere (Col. 1:28-29).

The best explanation therefore is a dispensational one: Granting the equal universality of salvation and healing theologically—that is, in the finished work of Christ in His Atonement on the cross—the actual experience of healing is not (even in New Testament times) enjoyed as universally as the grace of salvation by those who believe.

6

Seven Kinds of Faith

One of the most crucial issues in this whole teaching revolves about the definitions and understandings of faith. What is faith? What are its limitations? How many kinds of faith does the Bible teach? If the faith teachers are right in their research, the Bible only teaches three kinds of faith: (1) natural, human faith or "head faith"; (2) supernatural faith dealt to us by God, in other words, the "measure of faith" (Rom. 12:3) which is a grace gift; and (3) the faith every Christian has by virtue of being a Christian. Certainly the Bible distinguishes between head faith and heart faith, and it is equally clear that there is a distinction to be drawn between God's ministry gift of faith and the faith every Christian enjoys by virtue of being a child of God. But the question is, does the Bible limit itself to these three kinds of faith? For some this may appear to be a rather inconsequential matter, but it is a pivotal point for teaching, because if there has been a confusion, for example, between ordinary heart faith and the God-like faith of Mark 11:22 that moves mountains, then people are being asked to practice an impossibility; they are being asked to work themselves up to a kind of faith which is a direct supernatural gift of God. No amount of confession, singing or praise can wring from God that which is His sovereign right to give or to withhold. Where this faith exists, nothing, including mountains, can stand in its way; it is as powerful and creative as God's own faith, but where it does not exist, it cannot be commanded.

Probably few words evoke so many different things to so many different people as the word "faith." Faith conveys a whole spectrum of meaning to people. In one sense every person has faith. As someone has said, "It is never a question with any of us of having faith or no faith; the question always is 'In what or in whom do we put our faith?' " For example, even the Communists exercise a kind of faith. They have great faith, even irrational faith, that the maxims of Marx, Engels and Lenin will one day come true. It may be termed a quasi-religious faith, because for them the writings of Marx and Lenin roughly compare to the Bible in their authoritativeness. A secularized kingdom of God is for them the kingdom of man where justice prevails. A kind of heaven without God exists in the future for them in the classless society. In other words, they have great faith that eventually the fruits of labor will go to the proletariat, even though this has not worked out yet anywhere in the world after some sixty years of Communism.

It can be argued that even atheists have a kind of faith. When I was doing graduate studies at the University of

Minnesota I studied under two of the country's great exponents of logical positivism. They were practicing atheists and even evangelistic atheists. They not only taught there was no God, they wanted others to join them. Their "good news" was "there is no God." Of course, God has another name for the "There Is No God Club." He calls it the "Fool's Club," for in Psalm 14:1 God says, "The fool has said in his heart there is no God." An atheist may be defined as a man who has no invisible means of support when his world collapses.

If even the Communists and atheists, then, have a kind of faith, what is faith? One definition states that faith is complete confidence in someone or something that is open to suspicion. Another states that faith is a leap into the dark. A little boy gave a bad name to faith when he defined it as "believing something you know ain't true." A more sophisticated, although cynical, definition defines faith as "chasing a black cat on a dark night in a black room that isn't there," but this type of faith is not our concern.

We want to consider biblical faith. In the Old Testament the word faith is used only twice: once in describing children in whom there is no faith and again an obscure verse in Habakkuk 2:4 that the apostle Paul made famous, "But the righteous shall live by his faith" (Rom. 1:17).

In the New Testament it is quite another story. The word faith appears approximately 253 times; and if we add to this list of references the words faithful, faithfully, faithfulness and faithless we add almost 50 percent more words to the general term.[12] In other words, faith is a topic of consuming interest to the New Testament writers. Over 200 times the word used is *pistis* meaning persuasion; in other words, credence, conviction (of a religious truth), with special reference to reliance upon God for salvation. Since the word *pistis* is used overwhelmingly throughout the New Testament and is by all odds its most popular word for faith, the context, not the word, must determine the meaning of faith in a particular passage.

There are at least seven different kinds of faith that appear in the New Testament: (1) historical faith, (2) temporary faith, (3) saving or justifying faith, (4) faith in God, (5) faith of God, (6) faith as a fruit of the Spirit and (7) ministry faith.

The Scriptures describe historical or purely intellectual faith. This is the general faith that the Christian gospel is true. A man may be baptized and, being brought up in the Church, finds the Church's doctrine generally satisfying and thus decribes himself as a Christian. This includes an assent to the creeds, belief in the doctrines and the acceptance of the moral structures of Christendom. But to paraphrase Billy Sunday, "Being born in the church no more makes you into a Christian than being born in an airplane factory turns you into a 747." This kind of faith is not real and vital. It is simply intellectual faith. To a degree, all three branches of Christendom have settled for this definition of faith as a minimal standard, but it is clearly a sub-biblical faith, because it fails to call forth the radical faith response Jesus and the apostles demanded.

Many people have a problem reconciling the kind of faith James describes with what Paul has to say about faith. James seems to be saying, "If you have faith it will produce works. I can tell by your works whether or not you have faith." On the other hand Paul seems to be saying,

"It is faith alone that saves. Anything added to faith is adding to Christ and if you add works to your faith, your faith is, in fact, in vain." How do we reconcile these apparently irreconcilable differences? Once we accept the fact that there are different usages of the word faith in the New Testament, it is not difficult to reconcile the two. James is describing historical or intellectual faith. In James 2:19 he is chiding them for a kind of faith which has not issued in any good works and he says, "You believe that God is one; you do well. Even the demons believe—and shudder." What kind of faith do the demons have? They are perfectly orthodox. They know all about God; but they have no heart faith and therefore are damned to an eternal hell. James says, "Even so faith, if it have not works is dead being alone" meaning that if your faith is no better than the faith of the devils, then your faith is insufficient.

Historical or intellectual faith, then, is simply a faith that has not made connection with the real power in Jesus Christ.

A few years ago I was working as personnel director for a wonderful friend, Steve Lazarian. Steve has one of the largest electrical contracting services in the Southern California area, and one day he took me out to a job. There he was conveying 33,000 volts of electricity to a new factory. In order to handle that amount of power Steve had to have a hole dug which was approximately six feet broad by four feet deep and eight feet long. It took all of that space in order to put in the various electrical circuitry that would wire that great factory. The cable was a huge affair. However, if the cable had been one foot short not a single light bulb could have been turned on. The cable would have been there, the plant would have been completed and capable of turning out great industrial products, but until that cable made connection nothing could be done.

Historical faith is faith that hasn't made connection. Or as an Australian friend says with his inimitable accent, "It's like the Rolls Canardly bus, it rolls down one side and can 'ardly roll up the other."

Or, to borrow another illustration, if I were to buy a brand-new, beautiful Cadillac Seville and I called you over to admire my lovely new car, I might say, "Look at this beautiful chrome; it has excellent paint—seven layers of it, in fact—and look at the interior luxury. This car has everything my old car had and more. There is only one thing wrong. It is heavier and therefore harder to push." You would turn to me and say, "Chuck, you idiot, don't you know that there is enough power in that Cadillac to take you anywhere you want to go—what do you mean, 'push the car'?" In other words turning the key on would put me in direct contact with all the power I could use. Historical faith is faith which has not yet turned the key.

There is another kind of faith which may be called temporary faith. It appears in the story Jesus tells of the four kinds of soil in Matthew 13:3-8, 18-23. Although this faith involves intellectual assent, it has emotion linked to it as well. It receives with joy, but it is a faith that has not counted the cost. The Scriptures say "it had no root in itself" (Matt. 13:21). That is, the seed actually fell on a rocky ledge and as a result it could spring up quickly. The Holy Land is full of rocky soil and many times during the rainy season one can see little flowers peeking up through sandy ledges. In this case the seed sprang up quickly because it could not put down a good root system. But when the sun came up the seed could not abide the ordinary pressures of sun and heat, and it quickly succumbed. This story shows us that it is possible to assent intellectually, to have an emotional response, and yet not to have surrendered the will, the hard, impenetrable ego, to the person of Jesus. The text tells us it "had no root in itself."

This is the faith we often see evidenced at evangelistic meetings where altar calls are given. People respond in an emotional way but they never follow through. They are sincere and even initially joyful, but the hard core of the inner man has never been penetrated by the claims of Jesus' lordship, and at the first sign of opposition they fade away. When it says that the soil has no root in itself, it means that the inner man, the heart, the ego, has remained hard and impenetrable to the good seed. This individual has never fully surrendered himself without reservation to the person of Christ.

Here the gospel is understood as that which supplies man's needs, but it is not understood to be that which costs a man everything. We have read His demands so many times that they have lost their potency, but His demands are total.

This man's faith is temporary because when opposition arises and persecution comes, he turns back. He cannot stand the heat. This kind of faith, then, has certain characteristics as well. One is that the emotional feeling wears off rather quickly. A honeymoon with the gospel is followed by a repudiation of the marriage contract. Secondly, the inner nature of the man is not really changed; and although he appears to have put on Christianity, that in itself is the problem. It has not become his total life but simply something he has added on to what he already has. A third characteristic which Jesus shows is definitive for temporary faith is that this kind of man has no enduring power in time of trial, and so his faith utterly fails in the crisis. A final characteristic is that this man is quick to become offended when his plans are thwarted; when God does not do as he anticipated, when he is disappointed by heaven, he turns back. This is temporary faith.

A third kind of faith with which the Bible presents us is saving or justifying faith. Here is where the problem between Paul and James can be resolved. James is simply talking about an intellectual faith in which there has been no heart change, while Paul is speaking of the third kind of faith—saving faith or justifying faith which always results in heart change. One may say that it is faith alone that saves, but faith that truly saves is never alone. This kind of faith is the faith by which we receive Jesus Christ as Lord and Savior of our whole lives. It involves the whole man. It is the kind of faith that arrests a man going in one direction and turns him 180 degrees around. Not only are his intellect and emotions involved, but submission of his will to the lordship of Jesus is complete. He comes under a new headship. The whole man is placed under new management, so that we may truly say Christianity is a totalitarian religion. It does not demand much of a man; it demands everything. Paul speaks most frequently of this kind of faith. In Philippians 1:6 he says, "Being confident of this very thing, that he which hath begun a good work in you will perform it until the day of Jesus Christ" (KJV). In

2 Timothy 1:12 he speaks of this as the faith that knows beyond all doubt. "For I know whom I have believed, and am persuaded that he is able to keep that which I have committed unto him against that day" (KJV). We may speak of the acceptance of this saving faith or justifying faith as the most important act of any man's life; not to distinguish between temporary faith and saving faith is to confuse and obscure the distinctives of the absolute demands Jesus made on us. Does the essential difference after all between a Christian and a non-Christian come to this—that a Christian knows he cannot make it without God, and the non-Christian hasn't come to that discovery yet?

One day I was speaking at a Youth for Christ meeting, and at the end of the session I was confronting one of those who had shown interest in the claims of Christ. A young man was sitting close by listening intently. After I had finished with the first person I was counseling, he said, "May I ask you a question? I have more or less done that and it hasn't worked." I said, "You have more or less done what?" He said, "I have more or less accepted Christ as my Savior."

It is clear that he was the victim of a theological misunderstanding. Can a person be more or less bitten by a rattlesnake, or is a man more or less married? I'd never heard anyone say, "I more or less got married last night." A man is either married or not married. Is a person more or less dead? Either he is dead or he is not. No one yet has ever received a wire saying, "Your Uncle Ebenezer has more or less died. On Tuesday we more or less plan his funeral, unless of course he doesn't remain dead." If it is true that one is either bitten or not bitten, married or not married, dead or alive, then it is also true that one is either a Christian or not a Christian. There's no such thing as a more or less Christian. A Christian is by definition one who has repented of his sins and submitted to the lordship of Jesus Christ.

Justifying faith also has certain characteristics. One of these characteristics is that often a man who has been truly born of God does things he doesn't want to do in the natural for the Lord's sake. His attitude reflects that of Jesus, "Not my will, but thine be done" (Matt. 26:39). One of the questions a man must ask himself is, "Who wins the arguments between God and me?" If a man wins all the time, it may be evidence he does not have justifying faith. A second characteristic is that it perseveres through the trials still believing in God even when the world wears a "God-denying" look. First Corinthians 10:13 tells us, "There hath no temptation taken you but such as is common to man: but God is faithful, who will not suffer you to be tempted above that ye are able; but will with the temptation also make a way to escape, that ye may be able to bear it" (KJV). That verse is only for those who have justifying faith. They are the ones who find their faith in God strengthened rather than destroyed by trials. The fourth characteristic is that this faith can confess the lordship of Jesus without a quibble.

Often when people lack assurance concerning their salvation, I ask them if they have ever accepted Christ as Lord and Savior. If they say, "Yes, I think so; I believe I have, but I still have no assurance of salvation," I say to them, "Reach for your Bible. Now turn to Romans

10:9-10. 'If you confess with your lips that Jesus is Lord and believe in your heart that God raised him from the dead, you will be saved. For man believes with his heart and so is justified, and he confesses with his lips and so is saved.' Now this verse clearly points out that we are to confess Jesus as Lord with our lips. Do you see that?"

"Yes."

"Are you willing before God and these witnesses to place your hand on that Bible and from the bottom of your heart say, 'Jesus is my Lord'?" Many people have come to assurance for their salvation by using this simple, powerful way of affirming their faith. Their public confession nails down their private belief. It takes both to complete the transaction.

There is a fourth kind of faith which exercises faith in God for miracles, healings, and exorcisms. It is a miracle-believing faith, "Jesus Christ the same, yesterday, today, and for ever." Or as Rufus Moseley said, "What Jesus was, He is. What He said, He says, and what He did, He does." Every time a healing transpires, every time a person is set free, every time a sinner enters the kingdom of God, we have a sign that the kingdom is among us. There is no sickness in the kingdom. There is no oppression in the kingdom. There are none who are lame, halt, or blind. Wherever the kingdom has fully come, no pain, tears, or sorrow remain. For the kingdom life is a life of absolute health, complete freedom, and endless joy.

This is where one of the mysteries of the kingdom confronts us. The kingdom is here; yet it is not here. It is among us; yet it is to come. It has come; yet it has not come. It is in the here and now; yet it is in the not yet. It is in a process of realization; yet it has not been completed. That means that you and I dwell in the kingdom in measure. It cannot be completely fulfilled until the King returns. Those who look for perfection in the here and now are doomed to disappointment: the kingdom has not yet fully come.

This was part of the frustration of the disciples who felt so keenly the difference between the kingdom Jesus brought and taught and the world in which they lived. They asked the question that has pricked the hearts of all of us at one time or another, "Lord, wilt thou at this time restore the kingdom?" There is within each of us who have been born into the kingdom of God a burning desire to see the kingdom restored, and we find ourselves continually frustrated by the harsh realities of the present life and the knowledge of the kingdom which is to be. There is in the present faith teaching a strong undercurrent of confusion at this point; this teaching either consciously or unconsciously holds that the kingdom can be fully here, now here, for everyone who exercises faith. This kingdom confusion does not recognize the frailty and "not yetness" of the kingdom's fulfillment in the groaning creation of which we are a part.

As Christians we need to face the facts—positively, and with great faith, but still we must face the facts before us—the kingdom is not yet "fully come." The world still groans and travails. We are still waiting for "the revealing of the sons of God." Creation is still in bondage and in a measure so are we. Not only is creation wounded and in mortal pain, groaning for its redemption, but so also are we, not yet fully redeemed, not yet fully healed, not yet fully "clothed upon." We wait for it. We wait for it in hope. We wait for it in faith. Nevertheless we still wait.

To act as though the kingdom has fully come when it is not yet here is folly. To tell people they are healed when they are not healed is not bold faith; it is presumption *that the kingdom has already fully come* and the basis of presumption is pride. No one ever crawled away from the presence of Jesus shouting, "I'm healed, I'm healed," when in fact he was not. It is a cruel doctrine indeed that says to a person who has prayed and not been healed, "You have no faith." How can this be a ministry of reconciliation?

Furthermore, if we take the James 5:14-15 passages as normative for New Testament church practice, the emphasis here is clearly on the *faith of the elders,* not the recipients of the ministry. "Is any among you sick? Let him call for the elders of the church, and let *them pray over him,* anointing him with oil in the name of the Lord; and the [their] prayer of faith will save the sick man, and the Lord will raise him up; and if he has committed sins, he will be forgiven." The recipient shows his faith by calling for the elders; the elders show their faith by exercising the "prayer of faith."

Many believing Christians will say, "I have all the faith in the world," and they mean it. They have complete faith that God can and will heal, but that is not the same thing as the faith of God. When we simply have faith in God we struggle to believe. We confess our healing and believe as best we can. Faith has become a condition of our mind. We positively look forward to what God is doing. We expect the Lord to heal. Our confession is positive. Our trust and our faith are in the God of miracles. We try and try to believe, but our faith lacks one quality—certain knowledge that God has worked.

We may define faith in God, then, as faith in the Lord for miracles without specific knowledge in this particular case that God will heal. There is no certain word spoken to our spirit. We have a *logos* from God, but no *rhema*.

I thought of my two friends with a nearly identical heart problem. Both were Spirit-filled Christians, both knew God could heal, both were positively oriented for healing, but God healed one through His own sovereign, miraculous power and the other was healed through the ministry of medical science. Was one of God and the other not? In the former case God had given me a *rhema*. In the latter I was expressing faith in the *logos*. In the first case I had an inexplicable knowing, a knowing that was beyond all knowing; in the latter a great hope and faith but no knowing. One was faith in God; the other faith of God.

This brings us to the fifth kind of faith, the faith of God. Dr. Charles Price's book, *The Real Faith*, was a great help to me in that it distinguishes between what I have called faith in God and the faith of God.[13] Faith in God tries hard to believe. It basically says, "If only I can work my faith up to a certain point, knowing that God is able and I have enough quantity of faith, then God will move that mountain." It is a sincere, trying faith, but it attempts the impossible. We can never move from faith in God to the faith of God. The faith of God is wholly God's business. We cannot add to it or subtract from it. We can only exercise it when it is given. Here language study helps us out.

The Greek language distinguishes between several kinds of genitives, but for our purposes we will consider two: the objective and the subjective genitive.[14] "The objective genitive expresses the object of a feeling or action and must be distinguished from the ordinary subjective genitive expressing possession."[15] The objective genitive identifies with the object, i.e., as "faith in or towards the object, Christ" (Mark 11:22). But the more usual way to translate the same passage and one that is equally valid grammatically would be to understand it as a subjective genitive, denoting possession which then translates not "faith in God" but "faith *of* God," i.e., God's own faith. The context determines the usage.

For example, the best translation of Galatians 2:20 states, "I have been crucified with Christ; it is no longer I who live, but Christ who lives in me; and the life I now live in the flesh I live by the faith *of* the Son of God who loved me and gave himself for me." It is not as the RSV translates it, "Faith in the Son of God," but literally "In faith I live, that of the Son of God who loved me and gave himself for me." Here it is exceptionally clear that the faith by which Paul lives is not at all his faith in the Son of God, but it is the Son's faith by which he lives. It is not my feeble faith that saves me; it is Christ's own faith that holds me. Paul is not expressing here how he manages to cling onto Christ despite the ups and downs of life, but how Christ's faith holds him and how the faith he lives by is really Christ's own faith, which is both strong and secure.

It isn't our weak faith that saves us, but Christ's strong faith on which we rely. This interpretation of Galatians 2:20 is further borne out by the context where Christ, not Paul, is the focus of attention. Christ lives in him, Christ's faith holds him, Christ loves him and Christ gave himself for him. At least one scholar sees every instance of Paul's use of "faith of God" as the subjective genitive,[16] that is, God's own faith.

Now let's get back to the distinction between faith in God and the faith of God. Mark 11:22 literally says, "Have the faith of God." God is in the genitive case, but it can also be translated "have faith in God" with equal grammatical justification. The whole question hinges on whether it is an objective genitive (God as the object of faith) or a subjective genitive (where it is possessive and represents God's own faith). The context must decide the question.

The occasion is the cursing of the fig tree. The day before Jesus had cursed the unproductive fig tree and as the disciples went out the next morning the fig tree had completely withered. They were utterly astonished.

"Look, Lord! The tree you cursed yesterday has already withered!"

Now I have seen many fig trees in Israel and the truth is these handsome trees simply do not wither overnight. They are hearty, beautiful trees, wonderfully suited to the hot, dry climate. Very little discourages them or their succulent juicy fruit. To this day, Israelis prize the fig. It was a miracle that this tree would wither so soon. But Jesus is not surprised. He is teaching once again the lesson He most consistently taught throughout the Gospel of Mark—the main principle He wished to implant in the heart of His disciples—faith.

"Look," Jesus is saying, "not only can you curse and wither fig trees in a single day, but if you have God's own faith, the faith of God, you can say to this mountain, 'Be taken up and cast into the sea,' and if you have the faith that has no doubts, it will be done'' (Mark 11:20-24). Now despite the fact that Jesus often used exaggerated language to express truth, a literal application still remains. Were the occasion necessary, and God gave a man His own faith, a man could literally walk up to a mountain and say, "The Lord wants you moved; be removed into the sea!" He would probably face a law suit by the earth-moving people for working without a union contract, because that mountain would be literally moved. That is how powerful the faith of God is.

One day in Kenya, Africa, I saw mountain-moving faith at work. I was working with ORU's World Action team carrying the good news of God's healing power to a wonderful, believing people. I have often wished American Christians would exercise this same simple, vibrant faith.

Oral Roberts was praying for people in the prayer line, and suddenly I saw an old lady barely shuffling up the long platform that led past Oral. She was literally inching her way along. I was thinking and half praying, "O Lord, please hurry her up! Oral doesn't like to wait and I don't want to see him lose his cool in front of all these people!" After what seemed a full half-hour she finally reached Oral. He prayed briefly for her and she began to walk, slowly at first, and then faster. Soon her crutches went up over her head. By the time she had reached the end of the platform, she was running. The crowd went wild and started to cheer. People were jumping up and down, shouting praises to God and laughing. I knew something extraordinary had happened, because of the crowd's response, but I didn't know why people were so jubilant. Then someone told me the story. She had no hip socket when she had begun that long ascent—only a wooden board strapped to her torso and leg. Her crutch served as a second leg. That is why she walked her snail's pace. God had given her a brand-new hip socket on the spot—a mountain-moving faith that worked!

As I began to think about men of God I had read about and the faith they exercised, I saw a pattern begin to develop. Rees Howells spoke of the "gained place of an intercessor." He believed that in a particular area of faith a man could pray and always expect to see God work. There was no guesswork in it. George Müeller exercised this kind of faith for his orphans. He had no doubt about it. God gave him a special faith that He would always supply for the orphans. Later in life Müeller said it took no more faith to trust God for 2,000 orphans than it took for the first few little urchins he gathered around his table at the beginning of his ministry. In that area he exercised the "faith of God." God would supply and God always did. But in other areas, such as healing, he did not always have success. Sometimes God healed and sometimes He did not. There he exercised faith in God.

Then I thought about my own life and calling to Israel. On January 25, 1965, after nearly a month of time in the Word, prayer and fasting, God sovereignly gave me a call to Israel. It was during an agonizing session of intercession that I have seldom experienced before or since. In a way it had its comical aspects. I am one-half Syrian; my father was born in Damascus and I was brought up in a home with virtually no contact with Jews. I can safely say that love for the Jews was not a primary principle of my father's instruction! So being called to Israel could hardly be construed to be dad's first choice for me, yet the calling has persisted. Despite a costly and nearly disastrous early attempt to go to Israel, years of great ministry fulfillment and satisfaction in other areas, discouragement by friends and relatives who simply cannot understand, and personal disinclination on my part to live in Israel have nothing whatever to do with the call.

I've lived in Israel; it's not Shangri-la. And yet, as I have often observed to Jo Ann, so sure am I of this call that were there a hundred wonderful men of God who dropped by to express their concern, "Chuck, it's no good; you're not called to Israel," I would turn to her at the end and say, "Honey, can you believe it? One hundred men of God—and all of them wrong!" This is the "faith of God." It has nothing to do with me. I didn't make it up, work it in, or sing it out. It is just there—a quiet, unruffled certainty that some day I will live in Israel and have a part in helping God's beloved people. It is faith that is entirely a gift of God that has been dropped into the center of my heart. Praying all night, going on long fasts, retreating to desert vigils, all have their place; but they simply do not bring about this kind of faith.

The sixth type of faith, fruit-faith, is a product of the Spirit's work in our lives. Galatians 5:22-23 speaks of this faith: "But the fruit of the spirit is love, joy, peace, patience, kindness, goodness, faithfulness, gentleness, self-control: against such there is no law." This has to do with character fruit, and has no direct connection to ministry gifts. A person can exercise miracle faith quite frequently and yet have little faith as a fruit of the Spirit operating in his life. This faith carries the meaning of faithfulness, fidelity and staying power. It has to do with being a faithful steward of what God has entrusted, "faithful to the end." It is the faith that characterized a young English Christian who, over two hundred years ago, was captured by the French in the terrible wars between France and England. Impressed as a galley slave into the French navy as a boy, he rowed constantly amidst the most depressing circumstances, living in the most primitive conditions, denied land-leave and the normal dignities of a human being, existing on dried biscuits and water until finally, worn out, tired, and old before his time, he was dismissed from the service. Drawing on his long experience, he wrote a book entitled, *Fifty Years As A Galley Slave*. In the preface he wrote, "I thank God for the high privilege of having served so kind and gentle a master as the Lord Jesus." He had the faith born of long years of suffering that made his hardships appear to be graces under the lordship of Jesus. That is faith as character-fruit.

A portion of this type of faith may come immediately upon conversion, but it never instantaneously matures, because it is a faith that grows out of being conformed to the character of Jesus. It grows through the ups and downs of life, through its storms and its perils, through its agonies and its ecstasies, through its trials and its temptations, through its pain and its sorrow, and at the end it still declares, "I thank God for the high privilege of having served so kind and gentle a master as Jesus." It is faith that has survived the death of a loved one, the desertion of a mate, the dereliction of children, the ingratitude of friends, the isolation of suffering and even its disappointments in God, while still witnessing its fidelity to the living Lord. This kind of faith does not come until an individual has had an opportunity to disbelieve God. Faith as the fruit of the Spirit cannot be claimed until a person has had a real opportunity to be unfaithful. This kind of faith is not tested until a person has a legitimate case against God; then he could presumably appear in a courtroom and demonstrate that God had apparently been unjust. For the basic idea of this kind of faith is fidelity, and fidelity is firm adherence to the person to whom one is committed. Job exercised this kind of faith. Satan had wished to test Job because God was bragging on him and his fidelity, his faithfulness. He said, "Have you seen my servant, Job? He's blameless and upright, he fears God, turning from evil."

Satan rejoins, "Really? Big deal! Look at all you have done for him. No wonder he serves you. Furthermore, you put a hedge about him and I can't get to him." God gave Satan permission to break down the hedge and in one day, Job lost 7,000 sheep, 3,000 cattle, 500 yoke of oxen, 500 female donkeys, and, worst of all, seven sons and three daughters. This probably represents the single greatest tragedy any man in the history of the world has suffered. No one could argue that Job received justice because, try as they would, none of his comforters were able to lodge legitimate cause for his disaster.

Although Job has always been considered a man of great patience, he must also be understood as a man of great faith, for out of the expressful agony of his insupportable losses, his goods, particularly his children, he exclaims,

"Though he slay me, yet will I trust in him: but I will maintain mine own ways before him" (Job 13:15, KJV). Here is the final test of faith. Job represents the ultimate tragedy but his response is perfect. "Though he slay me, yet will I trust in him."

What God is after is "though and yet" believers. Though tragedy occurs, yet they trust. Job had lost everything; everything, that is, except a body full of painful boils, three miserable comforters and a bad-advice wife, who told him to curse God and die.

It is hard to tell what hurt more, the boils or the comforters. Although Job had lost everything, he retained his most valuable possession—his faith in God. Someone has said, "The only real tragedy that can befall a Christian is his loss of faith in God."

Here is the lament of Habakkuk 3:17 and 18. The prophet describes a horrible drought: fig trees which will not blossom, with grapevines shedding their grapes, fields barren of food, with the sheep, goats, and cattle dying in the fields. Although he is flat stony broke, his response is, "Yet I will rejoice in the Lord." He, too, was a "though and yet" believer.

God is in the process of calling forth a band of marching soldiers who can say with Paul, "I am sure that neither death, nor life, nor angels, nor principalities, nor things present, nor things to come, nor powers, nor height, nor depth, nor anything else in creation, will be able to separate us from the love of God in Christ Jesus our Lord" (Rom. 8:38-39). The Christian whose life is marked by this kind of faith in the midst of death, losses, and ill health, still says, "I trust in God." This is faith that is fidelity no matter what the consequences, this is a faith that outlasts even life itself. It is a fruit of the Spirit. Faith that fixes its object in God himself, and not in what He does.

The seventh type of faith is ministry faith and it is well outlined for us in Romans 12:3-8. There it says, "For I say, through the grace given unto me, to every man that is among you, not to think of himself more highly than he ought to think; but to think soberly, according as God hath dealt to every man a measure of faith. For as we have many members in one body, and all the members have not the same office: so we, being many, are one body in Christ, and every one members one of another. Having then gifts differing according to the grace that is given to us, whether prophecy, let us prophesy according to the proportion of our faith; Or ministry, let us wait on our ministering: or he that teacheth, on teaching; Or he that exhorteth, on exhortation: he that giveth, let him do it with simplicity; he that ruleth, with diligence; he that sheweth mercy, with cheerfulness" (KJV). In this passage of Scripture we are told that God has allotted to each man a measure of faith. It is quite comparable to the message God gave to Joshua many years before when he was about to take possession of Canaan. God had given him the whole land.

Can you see Joshua?

"Joshua, the whole land is yours."

Joshua seems lost in reverie.

"Joshua, the whole land is yours."

"I know, Lord, I know."

"Well, what are you doing with that silly grin on your face?"

"I'm just thinking, Lord, how nice it was of you to give

me all this land. I'm just going to sit here and wait for it to happen."

"Joshua, you misunderstand me. It's not yours until you walk it out. You don't get one foot more than what you walk on. Only what you personally take is yours." That's the way it is with our ministry gifts. God has given us the capacity, but we only get what we appropriate.

This is the thought here. You may have a particular ministry gift, but you must exercise the faith for it to come forth, for only what a man takes of the territory God has assigned to him becomes existentially his.

This passage is also instructive as to who comprises charismatic Christians. Verse six points out that we all have grace gifts, *charismata*, but they differ. Paul seems to be saying that every Christian is a charismatic Christian, but the only difference is in what kinds of gifts are manifested. Not only are they more spectacular gifts, such as prophecy, but also gifts of serving, waiting on tables, teaching and showing mercy. Even the gift of exhortation is a grace gift of the Lord. It is interesting to note that three things seem to stand out in this passage. First, every ministry gift is God-allotted; God is the initiator and giver of all the gifts. There is no room for one to call forth his own gift; it is of God's choosing. Secondly, all the gifts are grace-gifts or charismata, not just the more exotic gifts; serving tables is as much a grace-gift, a charismata, as prophesying or speaking in tongues. Therefore, biblically all Christians are charismatic Christians. And lastly, ministry gifts are an exercise of faith, a call for divine-human cooperation. No matter what the territory may be that God has assigned to a gifted person, he receives no more than what he exercises faith for.

The seventh kind of faith is ministry-faith. This is described in Romans 12:3, 6-8. "For by the grace given to me I bid every one among you not to think of himself more highly than he ought to think, but to think with sober judgment, each according to the measure of faith which God has assigned him. . . . Having gifts that differ according to the grace given to us, let us use them: if prophecy, in proportion to our faith; if service, in our serving; he who teaches, in his teaching; he who exhorts, in his exhortation; he who contributes, in liberality; he who gives aid, with zeal; he who does acts of mercy, with cheerfulness." Several observations need to be made about this passage. First, Paul is asking every Christian to make a clear distinction between faith and presumption. If a man thinks more highly of himself than he ought, he is presumptuous and this is not true faith. Second, it is clear that each Christian has a measure of faith and a ministry gift from God. Everyone has something he can use for the body. Thirdly, no distinction is made here between the so-called charismatic gifts, such as prophecy, or the noncharismatic gifts, such as teaching or exhortation. All the gifts of God are *charismata*, and therefore it can be inferred that the distinctions we have arbitrarily drawn between charismatic Christians and noncharismatic Christians cannot be sustained by Scripture. All Christians, by virtue of being in Christ, are grace-gifted, and therefore charismatic. Certainly Paul is not setting out an orderly procession of gifts descending in importance starting with prophecy and working down to acts of mercy. Done in faith, acts of mercy are fully as important as prophecy. All the gifts operate by faith. None can exist apart from an act of faith.

Lastly, Paul is clearly describing here ministry gifts for the body; it is to supply the body's needs that these gifts appear at all. "Let all things be done for edification" (1 Cor. 14:26). The gifts must operate by two criteria: the measure of faith God has given, and the measure of use to which we put them. There is a Godward side and a manward side. God gives the "measure," but man must exercise his "measure" within the territory God has assigned to him.

Let me review the seven types of faith found in the New Testament. Although the word faith was scarcely used in the Old Testament, it abounds in the New. The most frequently used word is *pistis*. When it is understood that the context determines the meaning, many wonderful truths fall into place. I found the apparent conflict between Paul and James was easily resolved when the context shows they were simply talking about two different kinds of faith. It also helped me to understand why some people who believe the same doctrines I do have no real knowledge of Jesus Christ. They have an intellectual faith without saving content. I found then that this saving faith is a gift of God and cannot be manufactured (Eph. 2:8-9). In the same way, I discovered I have no power to turn my confidence, trust, and general faith in God for miracles, signs and healing into the faith of God by any pious act of my own. I cannot confess it into being; I cannot work it up; I cannot create it. I simply acknowledge it and exercise it as God gives direction.

It is clear that those who teach "confession brings

possession'' have blurred the distinction between ''faith in God'' and the ''faith of God.'' Many people have come into unnecessary condemnation and even total loss of faith because this great Bible truth has been obscured. This is a clue to one of the major problems facing all of us who pray for the sick. The sixth type of faith is the fruit-faith of the Spirit who produces in us the character of fidelity and faithfulness no matter what the circumstances are. The seventh type of faith is a ministry faith, the results of God's gift and man's use.

7

The Faith Theology

One of the most rapidly spreading teachings abroad in the land today focuses around the "faith message." Congregations who hear this exciting message explode with enthusiasm and fire. Numbers grow astronomically and the congregations are positive and alive with praises to God. Positive statements are heard throughout the congregation where in truth "seldom is heard a discouraging word," and when that word is heard, it is promptly rebuked.

Schools teaching this doctrine are equally successful. Each year student enrollments continue to expand and increase, and no end is in sight. Once one accepts the full implications of these teachings and realizes he need never be sick, poor or die prematurely (some say they do not expect to die until 125 years of age), a feeling of tremendous euphoria emerges. It becomes a contagious enthusiasm enkindling hearts not only with hope, but with a certainty that what God promised will always take place. Faith is not a mysterious something that ''some could have and others could not obtain . . . unbelief or faith are available to every man'' (Kenneth Hagin, *How Faith Comes,* p. 1).

This is good news indeed. If I only learn how to exercise my faith, my rights as a child of God, I can enjoy perfect health, perfect peace, and perfect prosperity. It is simply a matter of applying the right laws in the right way. It is what I do that counts.

It is certainly true that the Scripture enjoins positive thinking and a positive approach to life. It is also true that people bring much of their sickness, trouble and pain upon themselves because they are guilty of wrong thinking and negative actions. Paul is very clear on this: ''Finally, brethren, whatsoever things are true, whatsoever things are honest, whatsoever things are just, whatsoever things are pure, whatsoever things are lovely, whatsoever things are of good report; if there be any virtue, and if there be any praise, think on these things'' (Phil. 4:8, KJV). Who can doubt that ''as a man thinketh in his heart so is he.'' There is an eternal spiritual law that what a man sows he does in fact reap. This remains true for the thought life, the word life and the action life. What a person believes often ultimately influences what he receives. If we expect good, good comes; if we expect evil, the bad generally shows up. Furthermore, we eventually become either negative or positive persons by our thoughts, our words and our deeds. The old adage still holds true: ''Sow a thought and reap a word, sow a word and reap a deed, sow a deed and reap a habit, sow a habit and reap a destiny.'' Any habits we can form that lead us to positive thinking, positive confession and a positive, praise-filled life are only to be welcomed and applauded.

Meditation in the Word, developing right attitudes toward our trials and tribulations and expecting God to bring victory out of defeat are positive expectations every Christian should enjoy. Practices such as saturating one's mind with positive promises of God, sowing good seed thoughts and speaking good words, developing positive thinking habits are all excellent biblical principles. One practitioner reports that he has been able to put in fifteen to sixteen hours a day, seven days a week, for many years as a result of practicing right attitudes.

We can only be grateful to God for the great influence positive confession has upon all of us, and for the tremendous effectiveness faith teachers have developed in spreading this truly good news of God's loving concern for our health and our prosperity.

Difference Between Faith and Belief

In examining faith teachings one quickly recognizes the careful distinction made between faith and belief. Although unsupported by exegesis, belief is distinguished from faith in that faith is "acting on what you believe" while belief tends to be more passive. One teacher explains that there is a difference between belief and faith, in that you won't get desired results from just believing until you do something about it.

Faith works locked into a knowledge of God's Word.

If you are ignorant of God's Word you can't exercise

faith. If God's Word says it, "Who hath blessed us with all spiritual blessings. . .," then all that is necessary is to apply this knowledge in an exercise of faith. This requires a good working knowledge of what God's Word actually says. Hence, there is an excellent emphasis on the study and memorization of God's Word. Unfortunately, the passages used are highly selective. For example, 1 Peter 2:24 says, "By whose stripes ye were healed" (KJV). Therefore, since healing occurred at Calvary and God has already done His part, all that is left for us to do is to exercise faith in the promise. Many teachers assure us that healing is a gift; all we have to do is appropriate it.

So the promise is unqualified. Thus, healing is equated with believing and acting upon the Word. When I act upon the Word, the consequence is healing.

Our problems with this teaching do not concern the merits and benefits of positive thinking, the emphasis upon right attitudes, or the need for a positive confession. It is rather with the sweeping generalizations that result from imbalance.

I am convinced that God meant every Christian to live a positive life of faith; that no matter what comes his way, he is to be ready for it. This is really the point of what Paul is saying in Philippians 4:13, "I can do all things through Christ which strengtheneth me" (KJV). One translation expresses the thought, "I am ready for anything that comes my way through Christ who strengthens me." The problem lies in universalizing a general principle. "Your condition will always parallel your confession." "What you say is what you get." "If you confess you are not feeling well, you will always be sick." "When you make a negative confession of faith you will receive nothing." If I were to take that last statement literally, then God has no breathing room nor do I. It simply is not true that I always receive what I confess. If this were true I would now be the country's greatest Bible teacher, a millionaire, a spiritual ruler over a city, a man of faith and power, a miracle worker, and a peerless leader among leaders. As a matter of fact, I am none of these things, though at one time or other in my life I believe I've confessed for all of them.

Nor is the reverse true. That is, that I never get anything from God when I make a negative confession. Oftentimes, I do catch myself in a "negative confession," but God in His mercy still visits me with good. Nor is it always true that if I doubt my healing, I always lose it. It may be granted as a general principle that positive confession brings forth positive results and negative confession negative results, but one cannot then claim this is true in every case.

In other words, let's reject the absolutist nature of this rigid formula-type theology and allow freedom to both God and man. God will not be bound by man's formulas.

A much deeper problem revolves about what faith action really is. Is it true, in fact, that every Christian has the faith to confess himself out of sickness into perfect health? Is it true that faith is nothing more than confessing what God's Word says? Is it true that we all govern our own faith and have great faith or little faith according to our own exercise of that faith? Is faith a kind of tree that grows inexorably onwards and upwards until it can confess and see miracles at will? If this is so, why is it that those in this ministry sometimes fail to gain physical healing for themselves? Is it always lack of faith?

Doubt

Faith healers have an explanation for this. The great reason we do not receive from God is doubt. Although a man may first act in faith, Satan can rob us of the answer by doubt. It is, therefore, exceedingly important to stop doubt at the threshold of the mind. Again, it is entirely up to you. There are no qualifications, no circumstances that could ever cause you to doubt again if you wish not to doubt.

The Christian is never to admit doubt, even in a small way. That would allow Satan to enter. Since "death and life are in the power of the tongue," we are enjoined never to use negative or doubtful expressions of speech. We are told not even to discuss problems with people who do not believe. One such "faith teacher" is positive that a man stricken with cancer of the hip and then healed, later died because he paid attention to the doubts of others who denied the validity of healing for today! Furthermore, some "faith teachers" claim that doubt and faith can never coexist at the same time in the same person. Evidently, although Jesus recognized the possibility of both faith and doubt coexisting in the same person at the same time ("I believe; help my unbelief" [Mark 9:24]), faith teaching does not. Fact is, we seldom experience pure faith. If Paul tells us, "I know in part," then how much more must our faith also be in part (1 Cor. 13:12)?

Two Kinds of Faith

This school of thought distinguishes between two kinds of faith: the faith God has dealt to every man in the body, and the faith we exercise. The first kind of faith is mentioned in Romans 12:3, "God hath dealt to every man the measure of faith" (KJV). In other words, God apportions a certain degree of faith to each member of the body for his place, purpose and function in the body.

This teaching suggests that we can receive healing by our faith or through gifts of healing or working of miracles (1 Cor. 12). The recipient's degree of faith has nothing to do with gifts of healing or working of miracles. But there is a kind of faith that enables us to determine what we will receive, according to those "men of faith." It is frequently tied in to one's obedience to specific formulas and rules.

No Medicine
Faith teachers vary somewhat on whether or not one can use medicine, but some definitely believe no medicine should be used after an exercise of faith. Teaching such as this may help to explain a tragic incident in the life of a good friend. A popular faith teacher was conducting a series of meetings in an Oklahoma town. The meetings were lively and exciting. As the singing grew in volume and enthusiasm, the teacher challenged the people to start dancing in the Spirit. Soon the whole congregation was dancing, praising God, and singing "Jesus, set me free." Suddenly, tragedy struck. A thirty-five-year-old, Spirit-filled rancher slumped to the floor. He had had two previous heart attacks. He had been healed from the first coronary, and a second heart attack had seen him restored through medical science. This time, however, nothing happened. A veterinarian attempted to give him artificial respiration, but the distraught young wife, Mary, pushed him away. She insisted faith alone would raise him. A

cardiac specialist was in the room and gently knelt beside the man, but was not permitted to touch the motionless figure. Mary became increasingly anxious and decided there was not enough faith in the room. To the hushed congregation she shouted, "Anyone that doesn't have faith, get out of the room!" Immediately the pastor and many others filed soberly out of the meeting and the cardiac specialist continued to kneel quietly beside the prostrate man; he was still not permitted to examine him. Mary kept insisting that faith and prayer would prevail, and only faith and prayer. Finally, after fifteen to twenty minutes of fruitless praying, Mary permitted the doctor to try for a pulse. There was none. Later she consented to calling an ambulance.

The faith teacher continued on with the service, interjecting phrases from time to time. "Our brother is not dead—the devil lies! Don't any of you tell me he is dead. He is not dead; he is alive and well!" Despite the fact that the doctor had pronounced him dead upon arrival, twenty or more from the service tied up the emergency rooms for over one and one-half hours praying for the resurrection that never came. Whether or not quicker medical attention would have saved his life is not known, but surely the folly of placing faith over and against medicine can be perceived. Bad theology is indeed a cruel taskmaster.

Those who teach faith versus medicine do not understand the two working together in a harmonious whole. They do not understand doctors and healers to be different members of God's one great team. Nor do they comprehend the different "delivery systems" God employs to make a person whole. Either you have faith or you use medicine, they believe. If you use medicine, you have no faith. So the Christian is left with a difficult choice of either bearing his suffering and pain in "faith," or seeking relief and healing through medicine in unbelief. This kind of either/or teaching ignores the neccessity of faith for healing in either of God's methods.

It is also true that when a man exercises faith in medicine, the results are sometimes dramatic. I saw a striking example of this in Africa some years ago when I noticed that everywhere I went aspirin was the most widely used medicine advertised. The claims that were made for it were clearly preposterous and I wondered that anyone could believe the advertising. It was widely hailed as a miraculous cure-all. The strange thing about it all was that it worked! I was left with the uncomfortable conclusion that the people's faith in the wonder-working merits of aspirin accounted wholly for its inexplicable success.

There is a place for doctors and there is a place for medicine. As Tom Smail puts it, "Medical healing bears witness to the providence of God in creation, providing within the natural order remedies and human skills for the ills of His creatures whereas divine healing bears witness to the operation of the Holy Spirit breaking through the limitations of the natural in a way analogous to what he did when he raised Christ from the dead" (Tom Smail, *Reflected Glory: The Spirit in Christ and the Christians*, p. 123).

Faith of God

In almost all translations, the passage in Mark 11:22

says, "Have faith in God."

Since we have previously shown this to be most likely a subjective rather than an objective genitive; that is, that God is the subject and author of faith and that it is His kind of faith, we might better translate this, "have the faith of God" or "have God-like faith" or "have God's faith." All would catch the substance of the idea.

The faith teachers also use this passage but fail to realize it is a very special kind of faith. For them, everyone has it. But the context shows that it is, in fact, an extraordinary faith, a faith God himself gives linked to miracles (1 Cor. 12), specifically mentioned by Paul as the summit of faith: "If I have all faith, so as to remove mountains" (1 Cor. 13:2a). They often contend that every believer has a measure of this kind of faith. This confuses the different kinds of faith which the Bible teaches. Let's look at the whole passage. And Jesus answered them, "Have [the] faith [of] God. Truly, I say to you, whoever says to this mountain, 'Be taken up and cast into the sea,' and does not doubt in his heart, but believes that what he says will come to pass, it will be done for him" (Mark 11:22-23).

The disciples had been amazed and wonder-struck by Christ's successful cursing of the fig tree. No other miracle impressed them more. Jesus had cursed the fig tree because it had produced no fruit. The next day, as they were passing by, the disciples noticed it was withering. It is in this context that Jesus spoke the preceding verse.

The key to an understanding of this verse is no doubt a little phrase, "in the heart." For the most part, our own faith waxes strong and wanes. It is almost never without doubt. Most of the time we are in the position of the honest father who had a demon-possessed son: "I believe; help thou my unbelief." Jesus is not speaking hyperbolically here; He is not talking primarily of the mountains of problems, doubts, or tribulations every man faces. He is speaking of actual, physical mountains that can be removed when this extraordinary kind of faith is exercised. Indeed, why not? The day before at His word the tree had ceased to live. Jesus is saying where this faith exists, anything God gives as His will for that situation can and will be accomplished. Jesus had good reason for saying this. After all, at God's word the worlds were formed; at God's word creation came; at God's word man was created. God's own kind of faith is a gift, a sovereign gift like the gift of miracle faith. It comes not by the will of man but by the will of God, but when this faith is really operative it is always effective, always powerful and always accomplishes the purpose for which it was given.

Healing Always Comes

If there is no healing can it be the problem lies in our receptivity? The faith teachers tell us that healing always comes but people, not understanding this, allow it to go by. The problem is simply lack of faith. One teacher explains that Matthew 13:15 means that healing always comes because God never fails, but some people can't see it due to lack of faith.

Faith in What?

In what is our faith to be placed? Is our faith in healing? Is our faith in salvation? Is our faith in the laws of prosperity? Is our faith in the exercise of our faith? In what or in whom is our faith?

I spoke to a beautiful young mother who had only one child and desired more. She had a cyst the size of an orange that had been discovered, and it may very well have rendered more children impossible. As she sat for prayer, she was anxious and teary-eyed. "I'm so confused because I believe in healing and God's promises to heal, and here I am with this terrible problem."

I asked her: "But where is your faith? Is your faith in healing or in the God who heals? Is it in the fact that God heals, or in the healing God? If I focus on the healing, I am bound to be confused, but if I focus on the living God, I can rest. I can relinquish even my healing into His hands, but I need to come to the place where I say with Job, 'Though He slay me, yet will I trust in Him.' This doesn't mean we do nothing—we do everything we can. We pray for healing, we consult with the doctors, but the final disposition is in God's hands. Are you ready to rest your whole case in God?"

Through tears she said, "I am ready." She poured out her heart to God in a beautiful way and received a great release. The anxiety was gone. The tension was gone. God was after her trust in Him and in Him alone. It was important for her to realize that the Lord alone was her source. The operation was a complete success and today she is a radiantly healthy young woman.

Our faith is misplaced if it is placed in faith principles; there is only one source to which faith points, the living God. As Corrie ten Boom says, "It is not great faith in God that counts, but faith in a great God."

The young mother's confusion was understandable

because she had been taught that Romans 10:9-10 gives us a formula for saying the word back to God in an exercise of faith that automatically completes the healing or gets an answer to the financial need involved. "Because if you confess with your lips that Jesus is Lord and believe in your heart that God raised Him from the dead, you will be saved. For man believes with his heart and is so justified and he confesses with his lips and so is saved."

These verses are not general verses on faith as we exercise them in the ordinary pursuits of the Christian life, but they deal specifically with the great theme Paul is developing: the theme of salvation and how it comes. Paul here is dealing solely with the how of salvation, not of Christianity in general. He finds that salvation really does divide into two parts: the inward belief of the heart and the consequent outer confession of the mouth.

"The beginning of the Christian life has two sides: internally it is the change of heart which faith implies; this leads to righteousness, the position of acceptance before God: externally, it implies the 'confession of Christ crucified' which is made in baptism and this puts a man into the path by which in the end he obtains salvation. He becomes *sodzomenous* (one becoming saved)." (W. Sanday and A.C. Headlam, *Epistle to the Romans,* p. 290.) The question, of course, is does healing in fact always come? Isn't there more to healing than saying the word? God works in "mysterious ways, His wonders to perform," and healing surely is one of those wonders. In God's dealings with men there is always mystery. We cannot squeeze God into our mold or pattern, no matter how appealing that idea may be. I think it was Einstein who said that we only know one-thousandth of one degree on a circle of 360 degrees. If that is true in the physical realm, how much more true must it be in the spiritual arena? However clever our formulas may be, or however biblical our deductions may be, we cannot put God into a box nor will He conform to our formulas.

And formula it is: wrong confession arises out of wrong believing. Wrong believing comes from wrong thinking. Wrong thinking is the result of thinking not yet brought into line with the Word of God. A wrong confession confesses how Satan hinders and keeps you from success. "A wrong confession glorifies the devil." A wrong confession admits one is sick when he is sick, weak when he is weak, and freely confesses problems, conflicts and defeats. It's seen to be a confession that God is a failure and that you are allowing Satan to have dominion over you. Naturally no one would want that to happen, so Christians are encouraged never to speak of pain, sickness, failure, defeat, sorrow or death. One wonders what unbelief Daniel was guilty of, that detained the angel three weeks (Dan. 10:2-3, 10-14).

One must ask, then, if Paul was not guilty of this heinous sin when he said, "Wherefore we would have come unto you, even I, Paul, once again but Satan hindered us." There it is in plain black and white. Paul was hindered by Satan and didn't know any better than to make this negative confession for himself and left it recorded for all succeeding generations to see. Nor was his "negative confessing" limited to Satan's power to hinder. He also confesses to being a fool, weak, despised, hungry, naked, and reviled (1 Cor. 4:10-13).

Where was Paul's positive confession? Why did he hunger and thirst? How is it that he was continually so poor and poverty stricken? Did he not understand that Christ had taken his poverty for him? Why did he allow himself to be treated as the filth of the world, and not stand up for his rights in the kingdom? Was he ignorant of the fact that a positive confession would have kept him from all this trouble? Or worse still, did he lack faith and thus suffer these horrendous deprivations? Didn't he care about himself and the effect his negative confession would have on the church? Was he some kind of masochist, bent on his own destruction? For what purpose did he go through all these things?

We are thus faced with a choice. Who then is correct? This suffering, despised servant of the Lord Jesus, or the "faith people" who categorically renounce such confessions as wrong believing and negative? Are we permitted to pick and choose selected Scripture verses to build a case or have we an obligation to be servants of the whole Word, seeking out the whole counsel of God? Even as I wrote these questions, in my mind's eye, I could see the redoubtable old warrior smile his half-sad smile, and he seemed to say, "Who now rejoice in my sufferings for *you*, and fill up that which is behind of the afflictions of Christ in my flesh for his *body's sake*, which is the church" (Col. 1:24, KJV). The purpose was suffering as an intercessor for the Church and for the furtherance of the gospel. Paul clearly taught a Christian realism that admitted defeat when defeat had come, and hindrance when there had been hindrance. Such a statement reflects the mysterious truth of Christian suffering that has not really been heard in our generation. Through it all there is a Christian "triumphalism," because He who is all in all and in us all will be finally reigning Lord of all.

It is small wonder then that certain teachers today tell us that if Paul had had the full faith message, if it had been revealed to him as it has been in this generation, there would have been no need for this suffering and this deprivation, this negative confession and the afflictions he so often bore.

Under the strictures of what a negative confession is, Jesus himself could be accused of negative confession. Frequently He referred to His impending death, and often spoke of how He had come to give his life a ransom for many (Matt. 20:28). To His followers, Jesus promised tribulation (John 16:33), revilings and persecutions (Matt. 5:11) and, to at least one of His disciples, death by crucifixion (John 21:18-19). No one, I think, would attribute to Jesus a causative effect for all of these terrible experiences awaiting himself and His followers by His "negative confession."

It follows, then, that if a negative confession causes all kinds of calamities which need not occur, a positive confession does just the opposite. The answer to prayer is in the confession of our mouths and hearts. That really means becoming, "God inside minded." This seems to make man's desires the focus of attention. It is not primarily what God wants, but what *we* want that really counts.

This kind of teaching would have us focus on our desires and not realize the higher purposes of God. Our desires, as we mature, should be what He would desire for us. Our desire should be that His will and His purposes be fulfilled in us.

Positive confession means you never confess that you are getting a cold or feeling ill or have a headache because of a great principle of faith: "What you say is what you get." Scriptural evidence for this is seen in the passages such as "Death and life are in the power of the tongue . . ." (Prov. 18:21). Proverbs 6:2 says, "Thou art snared with the words of thy mouth, thou art taken with the words of thy mouth" (KJV). The whole passage reads, "My son, if you have become surety for your neighbor, have given your pledge for a stranger; if you are snared in the utterance of your lips, caught in the words of your mouth; then do this, my son, and save yourself." Once again the context is the clue to the meaning. Here Solomon is simply stating that if a man has signed the bottom line for a stranger or a friend, he has already become ensnared by his words and needs to get himself released as quickly as possible (Brad Young, *Scriptural Confession "Jesus is Lord,"* p. 7).

This is not to deny that there is power in words. It is simply to deny that this text teaches that mere verbal utterance has the power of life or death. By neglecting contextual, scientific exegesis, people are brought into bondage to Scriptures which do not teach what they think is being taught.

This is how it works in divine healing. The secret is to act on the Word because you have what you say; saying, "I'm sick" releases a spiritual force that makes you even sicker. When you exercise faith in your feelings, it cancels out your body's natural healing powers, and since faith must be based on the Word and not on your actual condition, your confession must be according to the Word. In other words, "I have been healed no matter how I feel," or, "I am well by faith," or, "No sickness touches me because by His stripes I have been healed." If this sounds like Christian Science, it isn't, at least in this particular teaching. Teachers carefully distinguish between the denial by Christian Science of the disease and their own teaching. Although they disagree among themselves at this point, some do not teach "I am healed" when in fact they are not. Others say that the force of the confession itself is the exercise of faith, but more moderate teaching says, "By faith in God's Word, I am healed." If this sounds a little strange, they admit that as well. To questions of whether or not this makes sense, they often respond that it's not sense; it's faith. If they mean by this that faith is irrational confession contrary to the facts and therefore "non-sense," I cannot agree. Faith must acknowledge facts. Faith cannot believe what it knows to be untrue. Presumption may; faith cannot.

Genuine Faith

"Confessing the Word" is a foundational principle, and without question it works in many cases. Many people are undoubtedly healed when they confess the Word. But the question is, what of those who are not? The answer, though distasteful, is applied universally and it in fact must be applied this way because of the interior logic of the theology. There is no intended cruelty or unkindness in the answer faith teachers give at this point, but their theology demands a simplistic answer. It is lack of faith. If people exercised the faith they have, they would be healed. Why? Because it says so in the Word. If it says in the Word that "With His stripes we were healed," then this is past tense; He has done what He can. It is now up to us to avail ourselves of the healing that is already there. Failure to exercise the faith every Christian has is therefore the reason for failure to be healed. People are hung on the horns of a cruel dilemma. If it is in the Word, and faith is the condition, and all Christians have faith, then each Christian is responsible for failure because *each Christian is responsible for what he does with his faith*. Failure to be healed must always come back to lack of faith. Since by their definition of faith every Christian has it, there is no way to escape conclusions heard so often by so many. "It's your own fault. You could have been healed if only you had exercised faith." It is important to note at this point, this is not lack of compassion nor mercy on the part of the spokesman. It is simply an application of bad theology. Many charismatics deny the necessity of a good theology, but it should be obvious to all by now that theology to a very large degree governs the counsel we give to the afflicted soul. Therefore, we had better make sure our theology is consistent with the full counsel of God.

General Word or Particular Word

One of the fallacies that appears in all of this literature is the failure to distinguish between a general Word of God and a particular word for a particular occasion. In the illustrations chosen to demonstrate faith, there was always a specific word from God for that particular occasion. For example, when the case of Joshua is used for a demonstration of the general principle that he moved at the word of the Lord, no one can gainsay it. Joshua and the children of Israel subdued Jordan by simply obeying the Lord (Josh. 6:12-16, 20). The walls fell outward, but Joshua did not take that as a mandate for forming marching committees to parade around other cities he took for the Lord. In those, it was the more tedious task of sieging and storming the embattlements. Joshua did not make the mistake of applying a special word universally.

It is also true that Peter and the disciples caught a great multitude of fishes at the word of Jesus, but again we have to note that it was a specific word for a particular situation. Peter did not work that into a general manual of fishing and write a bestseller entitled *How to Fish at the Master's Word*! He knew it was a particular word of the Master for a particular occasion, and therefore had the good sense not to universalize it.

Nor did Naaman, the leper, return home after he had been healed from leprosy at the word of the prophet, following seven dips in the Jordan, to form a Lepers' Pilgrimage Society to make annual trips to the Holy Land for the purpose of receiving healing. God's particularized word, His *rhema*, always worked 100 percent of the time, but we must never fail to distinguish between a specific word and a general principle. Failure to do so catches us in the trap of blaming the poor sufferer when healing does not come.

God in a Word-trap
A second fallacy of this theology encapsulates God in a word-trap. God is no longer the free Lord of the universe,

who does according to His will in the council of heaven (Dan. 4:35). Rather, He is bound to the words of a book and becomes the captive of His Word rather than its Creator. Certainly the Scriptures are the Word of God, but they are dead and lifeless without the energizing power of the Spirit and His quickening of the Word to our lives. Christ is still Lord of the Scriptures.

A Theology Without Mystery

Theology always lives within the realm of mystery. No theologian can escape the mysterious ways of God, the capricious ways of the Spirit. Years ago Karl Barth wrote about the "strange new world" of the Bible. Theologians often note the strangeness of the men, material or resources He chooses to use. Theology is a peculiar science because, when it is most true to itself, it prostrates itself in humility, prayer, and adoration. True theology is a theology of prayer, and in the presence of the living God one adores; he never wholly understands. Any theological system that makes demands on God that are causative—that guarantees God will always act in such and such a way due to certain prayers repeated or rites performed—is bound to eventual failure. It is, in fact, magic. God is God, and man is man. Any theological formula that demands I always have food reckons without the Paul who went hungry. Any theological formula that demands God to always prosper me reckons without the evangelical poverty of the apostles and the early Christians. Any theology that demands God to always heal reckons without sick Trophimus or weakened Timothy, who needed wine to strengthen a sick stomach, or an aging Paul who was ill during the time he founded the church at Galatia.

This is not to say that the Church does not owe a tremendous debt to these teachers because of their great emphasis on positive faith and a God who answers prayer in the now. In a wholly negative world, this is a refreshing and needed message. The early apostles were the most positive people in the world, but it was not an easy "triumphalism" that guided them in escape from the tragedies of life by denying they existed, but a wholly realistic appraisal of life as a pilgrimage, a soldierhood through life's ups and downs in which Christian poverty, persecution and suffering were the hallmarks of the mature Christian, who was always being urged to take his share of hardships for the sake of the cross (2 Tim. 2:3-4). New Testament theology is an "in spite of" theology. It simply proclaims that "in spite of" life's sufferings and hardships, Christ triumphs, Christ reigns, Christ rules.

A Man-centered Theology

Easy "triumphalism" is a man-centered, not a God-centered, theology. The emphasis here is on what God can do for man; what the believer can demand and get; what is in it for the Christian. In this limited sense it represents a truly liberal theology centering on man—his desires, his ambitions and ultimately his world—rather than on God and His demands upon man. One of the distinguishing marks of liberalism is that it exalts man in his powers to change a world that grows progressively better. Following the heritage of Schleiermacher, the father of modern theology, we must recognize this tendency in the present tradition as anthropological theology; that is, an emphasis in theology that makes man "the center and measure and goal of all things" (Karl Barth, *Church Dogmatics*, Vol. I, Part II, p. 293).

It is a lonely Christian life indeed if what I want is the primary consideration. In fact it is a terrifying thought to be "Master of my fate, captain of my soul," particularly if I believe that God has left it all up to me. I frequently want what is not good for me, what will harm me, and sometimes that which would ultimately destroy me. I remember Oral Roberts voicing this thought one day. He said, "If it were not for the men around me, I would have destroyed myself long ago." The Bible gives us some horrifying examples of men who got exactly what they wanted, but the consequences were tragic.

Hezekiah was a righteous man, one of the greatest kings Israel ever produced, responsible for one of Israel's greatest revivals. The time came for him to die. Like us, he couldn't accept the decision; he wept bitterly, he prayed, he recited his many good works to the Lord. What added potency to his crisis was the fact that in the Old Testament death was shunned as the final horror because men did not have a resurrection hope. "The dead praise thee not." But the Lord heard and against His better judgment granted the answer to Hezekiah's prayer. Hezekiah didn't pray, "Not my will, but thine be done." He wanted his will—period! He got it; but during the fifteen years of extended life, he fathered Manasseh, a Caligula-like monster who almost destroyed Israel with his idolatries (Isa. 38, 2 Kings 20:24). He was, in fact, the worst king Israel ever had. What a dismal price Hezekiah paid to get his own way. And the tragedy was that all Israel suffered on his account.

Israel, too, demanded her way in the wilderness. The people were tired of manna, God's provision. They wept bitterly, longing for the leeks and garlic of Egypt, so God granted them what they wanted: a full month of eating quail until it "came out their nostrils." What a price they paid for their lustful gluttony! A great plague burst out against them, and many of them died. The Scriptures take cryptic note of the incident, "And he gave them their request; but sent leanness into their soul" (Num. 11:1-35, Ps. 106:15, KJV).

Christian theology must begin and end with its attention firmly fixed on the Word of God with a commitment to contextual, scientific exegesis; that is, an exegesis of the Scriptures that pays the closest attention to the context of the passage. It is scientific in the best sense of the word, in that it allows the text to speak for itself, thus modifying, clarifying, and illuminating any previously held ideas as to what the text may mean. We need a theology today that is both strongly theocentric and Christocentric. God has spoken and we need to hear His Word, not only the passages upon which "we can stand," not simply the "positive faith" verses, but upon the whole counsel of God.

The other day I heard a radio speaker give a "success formula" to his listeners. He asked them to repeat it after him. It went something like this: "Everything I touch will succeed; I cannot fail, because I have God in me, and God cannot fail. Nothing I touch can fail. Everything I touch will succeed. Failure is unknown to me." One could dismiss such impious drivel as theological nonsense, if it were not for tragedy that many sincere Christians swallow this line of thinking—hook, line, and sinker—and wonder then at the obvious failures. In such a theological framework, where I decide what I want to do and then call God in to get it done for me, it is easy to see how God is reduced to a celestial errand boy and how He makes a most convenient scapegoat when my plans don't succeed. Since I can't fail it must be God who failed. Such an egocentricity can hardly be dubbed Christian. To the contrary, the whole New Testament bears witness to the basic awareness—"We have met God, we have heard His word, that is the original and ultimate fact. The movement of thought here is not from below upwards, but from above downwards" (Barth, *Church Dogmatics*, Vol. I, Chap. 2, p. 21). To Barth's words we might add that having met Christ we know no alternatives but to submit to His Lordship. In this area, this theology represents an unwitting return to the old liberal theology that exalts man at the expense of God. A man-centered theology must ultimately fail, because truth finally triumphs; and the truth is, God is not here for our convenience, we are here for His purposes.

God's Sovereignty Questioned

Abroad in the land today is an increasing suspicion that "a robust faith in the absolute sovereignty of God is bound to undermine any adequate sense of human responsibility. Such a faith is thought to be dangerous to spiritual health because it breeds a habit of complacent inertia" (J.I. Packer, *Evangelism and the Sovereignty of God*, p. 10). The controlling factor in life is not man's handling of any given situation, but God's plan for it. This is what Jesus saw so clearly. His whole life was lived in the knowledge and execution of the will of God. It was not that He was a will-less being so drawn up into God that He had no will of His own: that would be to deny His true humanity; but it was that His will was always consciously and carefully brought into line with the will of God. His own will remained healthy and powerful until the end at Gethsemane, where he prayed for another way out but finally submitted in that ultimate surrender, "Not my will but thine be done."

How is it that Jesus never had a failure in His healing ministry? If Jesus entered fully into our humanity, as the orthodox creeds have rightly confessed, could He not have failed in His humanity? Why did He not fail as well as we? This controversy parallels an ancient controversy resurrected in a different form. For years the Church argued about whether or not Jesus could sin. If He were human, the possibility of sinning had to be there, but if He were divine, how could He sin? So the Church solved the problem by stating it in a beautiful paradox that retained the mystery of His divinity while giving full expression to His humanity. It never really attempted to bring the two scriptural truths together; it simply said, "As a human He is able not to sin, and as divine He is not able to sin."

The same principle applies to His healing powers. As truly human, the possibility of failure must be faced, but as God He could not fail. I am convinced that the healing ministry of Jesus related much more to His humanity than to His divinity. Otherwise, our emulation of Him would be futile. We can imitate Him in His humanity, but not in His divinity. To Him was given "the spirit without measure."

The secret of Jesus' success was His fidelity to the Father's will and His perfect knowledge of that will. We lack both; but to the degree we know His will and do His will we can repeat the very deeds of Jesus—healing for healing, miracle for miracle, exorcism for exorcism. Jesus states His secret in John's Gospel. Jesus said to them, "Truly, truly, I say to you, the Son can do nothing of his own accord, but only what he sees the Father doing; for whatever he does, that the Son does likewise" (John 5:19). Jesus did nothing but what He saw the Father already performing.

He did not heal the multitude of invalids at Bethesda because He did not see the Father doing it. He did not heal everyone within the range of His ministry because the Father was not acting. When the Father moved, He moved. When the Father was silent, the Son did not presume. Perfect foresight brought forth perfect results.

The charismatic movement desperately needs a new emphasis on the sovereignty of God. The famous first answer in the Westminster *Shorter Catechism* is entirely appropriate. "Man's chief end is to glorify God, and (by so doing and in so doing) to enjoy Him forever." The glory and praise of God should be the consuming passion of our hearts in the here and now, and the whole purpose of our existence should be to please God in time and eternity. If God has a plan for my life, it is not my prerogative to look about, decide what I want, and then order God to perform it. It is my whole duty to seek out God's will for my life, search out His plan, and then move in His plan for me, not my plan for Him. As John Calvin so well said, "Accordingly, the Christian must surely be so disposed and minded that he feels within himself it is with God he has to deal throughout his life." If there were to be allowed to me one verse in the life of Jesus to covet passionately, it would not be to be endowed with His miraculous powers, His amazing authority, or His speech. It would simply be the singular testimony He bore of himself, "I do always what is pleasing to him" (John 8:29). As Charles Simpson has said, "If you want to get along with God, you had better stay off His throne."

Problem with Man-centered Gospel

The problem with a man-centered gospel is that it never draws the individual out of the nobility of God's ultimate intention. It fails to recognize the necessity for something other than the self as the focus of life. It is not my Cadillac, my health, my money, my success, my fame that ultimately counts, but how do these things contribute to the furtherance of the kingdom of God? As Calvin has said, "We are not our own: but not our reason nor our will therefore sway our plans and deeds; we are not our own. Therefore let us not set it as our goal to seek what is expedient for us according to the flesh. We are not our own; insofar as we can, let us therefore forget ourselves and all that is ours" (John Calvin, *Institutes of the Christian Religion*, Vol. I, p. 698). The Christian never progresses beyond the cross. In my youth I used to grow bored and weary with preachers who endlessly preached the cross. I used to say to myself, "Why don't they go deeper? Why don't they feed me? Why all this talk about the cross and suffering? I'm sick and tired of it. I want something more!"

Since then I have learned that to go beyond the cross is to backslide. It is to stand in need of repentance, for it is proof positive I have left my first love. The cross is God's reminder to me of the ultimate prayer of the Christian, modeled by Jesus: "Not my will, but thine be done."

The difficulty of an adequate choice for the Christian is the point of a famous remark by a Russian writer: "A friend once wrote to Turgenev, 'It seems to me that to put oneself into second place is the whole significance of life.' To which Turgenev replied, 'It seems to me that to discover what to put before oneself in the first place is the whole problem of life' " (Quoted in Titus/*Ethics For Today*, p. 201). For the Christian this is an already answered question because Jesus made it clear: "Seek first the kingdom of God and His righteousness and all these things shall be added unto you" (Matt. 6:33). The emphasis throughout this theology is on what man can get from God. It is as though God had given to man a great sovereignty—God's plan was that man's plan should succeed. There is little emphasis in any of the literature upon the plan of God for your life other than that God plans freedom from sin, sickness, disease, poverty and death for each Christian. There is not a single instance in the Gospels where Jesus healed without some physical, tangible evidence of that fact.

Nobody was healed by Jesus without a real change occurring. However, for teachers to tell people they have been healed while the years roll by without any physical change is bad enough; but then to claim that this non-healing is the healing Jesus promised is not faith; it is presumption. Further, to be told that healing always comes, the fault is ours for not receiving it, can only result in the worst kind of spiritual bondage and condemnation.

An Act-Consequence Theology

Addicted as it is to the recitation of certain formulas which are always alleged to work, it judges the amount and quality of faith directly by results or consequences. If I fail to get my healing, for example, it is evident I have not acted on my faith; for if I had, my healing would be in evidence. Since it is not (*consequence*), it is clear that my *act* (exercising faith) was insufficient. No matter how one protests the naming of the other factors such as the frailty of human flesh, inevitability of death, or God's will, the answer is always the same: lack of faith. It is an act-consequence theology.

The book of Job deals devastatingly with a persistent theme in all religious thinking, the act-consequence principle. If I do certain acts, certain consequences inevitably follow. The converse also holds true. If certain consequences appear, I must, in the nature of the case, be guilty of certain errant deeds. Job's comforters represent this kind of thinking, par excellence. Job had suffered calamitous consequences; therefore, he must have sinned. God clearly disavowed this type of theological reasoning—"You have not spoken of me what is right" (Job 42:7). But this type of thinking still exists today. My mother told me of a healing incident with two dear and godly friends who were given to an act-consequence theology. Mother suffers from cataracts on her eyes that have not yielded to prayer, the use of magnetic fields or medicine. After prayer for her, her friends explained to her their understanding. "Dear, it really boils down to this. If you aren't healed, it's your fault. It's due to your lack of faith because God's Word has to be true." Mother said, "If I were to say, 'But I don't believe that way,' they would simply look back on this as a rejection of truth."

Another Gospel?

Some of the teachers believe they have passed beyond the pale of human illness and some believe they will be almost immortal, living on to be 120 years old or more. Carefully, they explain that the devil may try from time to time to put something on them, but it isn't going to work because they won't sign for the package. Certainly, one can commend the courage of any man to claim he will never be sick, but one wonders at its wisdom, even though the teachers have learned to repeat the formulas of faith. Though they believe they have been delivered from the Adamic curse, and are no longer subject to the ups and downs of life that plague you and me, it is a difficult thing indeed to predict the future. It is almost as though a new super-race had emerged, a race of Christians who will never know another day of poverty, another day of disease or sickness; it is no wonder Christians all over the world are anxious to become partakers of such blessings.

There's no longer a need to crucify the flesh; indeed my wanting a Cadillac and confessing its possession can be an act of faith. "If you have faith for a Chevrolet, drive a Chevrolet; but if you have faith for Cadillac, drive a Cadillac." No need to seek the lowly way, because God wants me to behave like a King's kid; and as everyone knows, King's kids travel first-class. That we are King's kids, no one denies; the question is, what kind of King? If it is true that the servant is not above his master, then I cannot complain if I have no more than Jesus, who had no place to lay His head. Under this teaching I no longer have to suffer privation, endure persecution, be thrown in jail, go hungry or thirsty, or suffer shipwreck for the gospel's sake. Jesus did it all for me. He became poor so I could become rich; He suffered so I wouldn't have to suffer; He was persecuted so I need not be persecuted; He had no place to sleep at night so I could live in the Hilton; He had to walk so I could drive an air-conditioned luxury car; He went hungry so I could be full; He was hot and dusty so I could enjoy clean showers and temperature-acclimated swimming pools. All this Jesus did for me. He died to make me comfortable.

What a fool I am then to hazard my life for the gospel's sake, to live moderately so that I can use my excess funds for missions, to crucify the flesh when God really wants to puff it up with new homes and bigger and better cars. What a fool I am to fast and pray, to beseech God to revive His Church, to take her from her deadly complacency, to become once again the suffering servant Church, binding up the world's wounds with her own resources. What a fool I am to spend days and hours in intercession and fasting on my face before God when all I need to do is pray once, because to pray more is to show "I have no faith." What a fool I am to be ready to don a martyr's crown or wrestle in the heavenlies with the unseen powers that are simple to exorcise, for "one believing prayer" will do it all.

Yet I take comfort that the problem is not new. Paul

could have been writing directly to twentieth-century charismatics when he said, "Already you are filled! Already you have become rich! Without us you have become kings! And would that you did reign, so that we might share the rule with you! For I think that God has exhibited us apostles as last of all, like men sentenced to death; because we have become a spectacle to the world, to angels and to men. We are fools for Christ's sake, but you are wise in Christ. We are weak, but you are strong. You are held in honor, but we are in disrepute. To the present hour we hunger and thirst, we are ill-clad and buffeted and homeless, and we labor, working with our own hands. When reviled, we bless; when persecuted, we endure; when slandered, we tried to conciliate; we have become, and are now, as a refuse of the world, the offscouring of all things" (1 Cor. 4:8-13).

Sovereignty Committed to the Church

One of theology's chief roles is to correct theological imbalance. So much emphasis currently has been placed on man's responsibilities, it was inevitable that sooner or later an incident such as the following would occur.

I had taken a series of meetings for a friend in St. Louis. The previous year he had come through some deep problems as gifted members of his staff were caught up in teachings he felt were foreign to the New Testament. They spent hours together in discussion. They prayed together. They sought the Lord together, but somehow the rift only deepened. They were simply unable to agree; they could not get it together. Finally, Bob blurted out what he felt to be a word of wisdom, "But you don't believe in the sovereignty of God!''

"You are right!'' the brother exclaimed. ''In the Old Testament God was sovereign, but in the New Testament He committed His sovereignty to the Church. We are now in charge; His sovereignty has been entrusted to us.'' I am sure not all the leaders of the faith teaching movement would agree with this, but if I really believed God had committed His sovereignty to an errant and fallible church, I'd pass sleepless nights worrying about the future. I'd wonder where I could find a sovereign God.

Paul's Illness

"As you know, it was because of an illness that I first preached the gospel to you. Even though my illness was a trial to you, you did not treat me with contempt or scorn. Instead, you welcomed me as if I were an angel of God, as if I were Christ Jesus himself. What has happened to all your joy? I can testify that, if you could have done so, you would have torn out your eyes and given them to me.'' Was Paul's failure to get healed evidence of his lack of faith (Gal. 4:13-15 NIV)?

The word for illness here is *astheneia*, which means disease, infirmity, sickness, weakness. Lightfoot translates verse 13 to say, ''on the account of an infirmity in my flesh.'' Paul had evidently never intended to preach in Galatia, but he was detained by an illness that made it impossible for him to continue on. It is possible that the old messenger of Satan who had buffeted him, who had literally struck him in the face, again attacked him, leaving him physically ill and exhausted (2 Cor. 12:7-9). Whatever it was became so visible that it was a trial to the

Galatians, and when he speaks of being treated with contempt or scorn, the literal translation is "to spit at." In other words, he was such an object of loathing that they could have spat at him in scorn, but instead they had welcomed him as an angel of God.

Yet out of this illness Christ brought forth a church that, humanly speaking, would not otherwise have existed. Had Paul not been ill, he never would have founded the church. No doubt Paul was disappointed by his sickness. Perhaps he too could not understand why he was sick when so much work remained to be done. No doubt his sickness reminded him that daily his strength was "made perfect in weakness" (2 Cor. 12:9). But the founding of the church at Galatia became the occasion of the expression of Paul's great revolutionary theology: The just shall live by faith alone. Developed first in the white heat of controversy in Galatia and later expanded into the magnificent book of Romans, considered by many scholars as the most important book of the New Testament, this far-reaching truth—later known as the Protestant principle—resulted from Paul's illness.

Here his illness promoted the glory of God. This is not to argue that God laid sickness on the apostle Paul, but clearly God permitted Paul's sickness for His own sovereign purposes. Surely the charismatic movement deserves the plaudits of all Christendom for emphasizing the great truth that God wills health for mankind, but perhaps in its reaction against those who have simply resigned healing into the hands of God's sovereign mercy, without praying in faith for the sick, or resisting the enemy, it has also neglected a legitimate truth. Sometimes

God does work illness to His glory. This was Jesus' point in correcting the bad theology of His disciples who felt that either the blind man had sinned or his parents. Jesus' words are instructive for us. "Neither hath this man sinned, nor his parents: but that the works of God should be made manifest in him" (John 9:3, KJV).

What was Paul's trial? The oldest tradition says that Paul was accustomed to violent and prostrating headaches. Another tradition says that, because Paul was blinded on the Damascus Road, a crippling disease caused a kind of running pus from the eyes that could have been ugly to behold. Paul's eyes were healed of their blindness but not of this condition. A third tradition says that Paul was, in fact, an epileptic and that he would take sudden seizures. Previously it was fashionable for liberals to interpret Paul's Damascus Road experience as an epileptic seizure. A fourth tradition says that he had contracted malaria down in the lowlands and had now come up to the high plateaus of Galatia to escape the marshlands where the malaria-bearing mosquitos dwelt. We cannot know for sure what the malady was, but that it was a physical infirmity there is little doubt. So a question arises, was Paul then backslidden? If he had been walking according to the faith message, would he not have been healed?

He is a man without the care of making friends, without the hope or desire of worldly goods, without the apprehension of worldly loss, without the care of life, without the fear of death. He is a man of no rank, country or condition, a man of one thought—the gospel of Christ. A man of one purpose—the glory of

God. A fool and content to be reckoned a fool for Christ. Let him be called an enthusiast, a fanatic, a babbler, or any other outlandish nondescript the world may choose to denominate him. But still let him be nondescript. As soon as they call him traitor, householder, citizen, man of wealth, man of the world, man of learning, or even man of common sense, it is all over with his character. He must speak or he must die and though he should die, he will speak. He has no rest but hastens over land and sea, over rocks and trackless deserts. He cries aloud and spares none and will not be hindered. In the prisons he lifts up his voice and in tempests of the ocean he is not silent. Before awful counsels and throned kings, he witnesses in behalf of Truth. Nothing can quench his voice but death, and even in the article of death, before the knife severed his head from his body he speaks, he prays, he testifies, he confesses, he beseeches, he warns, and at last he blesses the cruel people.

Was such a man as this in a backslidden state and is that why he fell prey to illness?

Paul had learned that although God wills health, we are not always healthy. Though God wills life, we will all die one day. Although God wills our good, evil sometimes overtakes us. Paul had learned the secret not of total health but of total contentment. He writes in Philippians 4:11, "I have learned, in whatever state I am, to be content."

My concern is for the thousands of people for whom the faith message has not worked, who are now far from God and some even actually disbelieve because their expectations were dashed. They applied what they knew, but a loved one died. They exercised faith, but another lies habitually crippled. They went to their leaders and were told, "It's your lack of faith. If you only had faith, this would not have happened."

Recently when I was in Lubbock, Texas, a fellow pastor told me of a church in the area in which an elder's wife had fallen ill. This church was thoroughly committed to the "faith message." When his wife fell ill, they threw him out. The logic of their theology carried them to that conclusion. If the man's wife is ill, it is obvious he is not exercising sufficient faith. If he is not exercising faith, he is not worthy to be an elder. If he is not worthy to be an elder, he should not be among us. What a cruel taskmaster bad theology is!

Christian Dualism

I do not use dualism here in the philosophical sense of two eternal co-existing principles, but in the practical sense of opposing principles locked in struggle.

For many charismatics a kind of practical Christian dualism exists; that is, God and the devil are about even with a slight edge being given to God. God is a good God who provides all the beautiful things of life: music, flowers, health, wealth, and all "the blessings of Abraham." Everything good comes from God; everything bad comes from the devil. Whenever a trial or a tribulation comes, the devil laid it on us. The Scriptures tell us, "Resist the devil and he will flee" (James 4:7). Therefore, when we see people in the middle of it, fighting poverty and ill health, watching their children wander away from God, vexed and perplexed by the course life has taken, feeling forsaken by God and by man, we can pretty safely conclude they haven't taken their throne rights, haven't demanded their inheritance as King's kids. Otherwise, bad things wouldn't happen to them. In fact, to believe God sends trials and perfects us through temptation is a deception. (Some of the faith leaders actually teach this.) Evil does occur in the lives of Christians, but it only comes because the believer fails to exercise his personal sovereignty over circumstances. The believer controls his world by his confession and exercise of faith.

The believer, then, is sovereign on earth and controls his world by right thinking, right conduct, right confession, and the right exercise of faith. You may be asking, "But how does this work? How can this be possible while we are still under the Adamic curse? Where is the theological basis for this belief?" This teaching says the curse of Adam can be nullified by the alert believer who knows how to apply the "blessings of Abraham," and that there is no middle ground. Believers who fail to do this are doomed to participate in life's usual ups and downs, and become burdened with the problems of the world. But it is potentially unnecessary for the believer to undergo the trials that beset the average man; in fact, to do so shows he has not utilized his "umbrella of protection." One wonders how this applies to the suffering church in Ethiopia, or the persecuted Christians of Amin's Uganda. One wonders how the "umbrella of protection" covers the Christians of China, or the untold millions of Communist Russia. If any such umbrella exists, it must be for the

United States alone.

One of the most intriguing questions the faith teachers need to address is the particularity of their doctrine. The gospel of prosperity must be limited indeed to a few countries of western Europe and the United States. Can you imagine the absurdity of preaching to the underground church in Russia that if they would only elevate the sights of their faiths, they could all be driving Cadillacs? Or can you imagine the blank stare a faith preacher would get from the "boat people" now escaping Vietnam by the thousands to be told they had only to exercise their faith and the good life would be theirs? They would be delighted with any kind of life at all. Or are we to assume that among these "boat people" there are no Christians? And upon what evidence would we test that hypothesis? If the situation were not so tragic, it would be wildly comical to imagine such an exchange.

The faith message is a local message; it can only be attractive in the most privileged parts of the world; it is a local message only applicable to 10 percent of the world at best; only the richest nations could furnish an audience for its teachings.

For theology to be any good at all, it must be universal. It must be applicable within terms of scientific exegesis any time, any place in the world. Thus faith theology is bad theology; it is not universally applicable. Were the glitter of our materialism less blinding and our own selfishness less tenacious, it would be obvious to us that Paul bears more kinship to the "boat people" than to King's kids going first class; the apostles would gravitate by nature of their own experience to the martyred Christians of Uganda faster than to American Christianity. One cannot help but wonder if Jesus had our generation in mind when He asked if He would find faith on the earth when He returned. How many will remain faithful when He replaces our baubles with a cross?

Of course the believer is delivered from the ultimate consequences of the Adamic curse through the redemption of Christ. It is certainly true, "Christ redeemed us from the curse of the law" (Gal. 3:13), but there is not the slightest indication Christians escape either the problems of the world or the final enemy, death, barring, of course, the Lord's return. In addition, the Christian is promised a special kind of tribulation: persecution for Christ's sake. Jesus says, "In the world you have tribulation; but be of good cheer, I have overcome the world" (John 16:33). It has been my observation that throughout history where the world gets thumped once, the Church gets thumped twice.

For many charismatics, then, God is the author of all that is good, and the devil is the author of all that is bad. When trials come, insoluble problems arise, or one of life's inevitable tragedies occurs, the average charismatic is ill-equipped to handle it. He desperately resists the devil; nothing happens. He enlists a believer's group to assemble more volume against the roaring lion. Evidently, there is a notion abroad that the devil can't hear very well, and if only we can amplify our voices to the decibels he understands, he is bound to flee. When that fails, he runs to his favorite teacher who tells him he isn't exercising his faith enough. He tries that, but the problem still exists. Next he invests time or money in the Lord's work, but things only grow worse. His crop fails, his faith fails, and the devil fails to obey and flee from him. Finally the bubble bursts. Satan has won; he has really won and faith is often shattered. Thousands of Spirit-filled Christians wander about today in a dazed state of nonbeing, not at all sure that "God is still on His throne," but absolutely convinced that they are no longer God's people of faith and power. A man caught in this dilemma makes one last and horrifying conclusion, "It may work for others, but it certainly hasn't worked for me." Of course, a corollary of that is, "God doesn't like me as well as He likes the other fellow."

Is there a word from God for such a sufferer? Is there any balm in Gilead to heal the battered soul? Does God have any comfort or reassurance to give?

He does. But at first glance it seems like cold comfort indeed. The truth is that God is in control of it all. His hand is on the evil as well as the good. He allows himself to be held ultimately responsible for the evil (not sin) as well as all the good and beautiful things of life. Listen to Isaiah's words: "I form the light, and create darkness: I make peace, and create evil: I the Lord do all these things" (Isa. 45:7, KJV). The Lord God permits all these evils to arise in my life and for precisely the reason some teachers disdain. It is to produce Christian maturity, Christian character, and to conform us to the image of Christ. If Christ learned obedience through the things that he suffered, how much more will we (Heb. 5:8)? The Christian may concede God "creates evil"; that is, in the form of natural calamities and disasters. But what of monstrous evil kings who only plunder, rape and murder? Isaiah didn't blink an eye at the moral implications. He says, "Behold, I have created the smith who blows the fire of coals, and produces a weapon for its purpose. I have also created the ravager to destroy; . . ." (Isa. 54:16). Job's maturity outshines ours. When everything was gone, his children slain, all his goods and cattle carried off, he simply commented, "The Lord gave, and the Lord [not Satan] has taken away; blessed be the name of the Lord" (Job 1:21). Peter Van Woerden lashed out at a "regular cult of Satan" he found among charismatics. "Don't say, 'How strong is Satan?' Don't give Satan that honor; God is sovereign" (Peter Van Woerden's sermon, July 9, 1978, Tulsa, Oklahoma). It is a timely word.

Plea-bargaining

When death stares us in the face, we often enter into plea-bargaining with God. Dr. Elizabeth Kubler-Ross discusses the characteristics of this type of prayer. First, a prize is offered for good behavior. Second, a self-imposed deadline is set. Third, an implicit promise is made not to ask for more if this one postponement is granted. What she does not mention is the horrendous consequences that follow when the request is not answered.

I had never really seen this process in operation until a friend introduced me to a woman in dire straits. Her husband lay terminally ill of cancer. She was somewhat acquainted with a church, but knew nothing of a personal commitment to Christ, so I was pleased and somewhat surprised at her eager acceptance of Christ on our first visit.

Her decision appears to be what she offered to God as evidence of her good behavior. The self-imposed deadline was the healing of her husband. Although she ardently desired me to pray for his healing, she was strangely reluctant to have me share Christ with him. All her energies were concentrated on her one great mission: the restoration of her mate. Her husband grew steadily worse. I tried to prepare her gently. "Sally, you know I believe in healing, but God doesn't always heal. The essential thing is that Tom come to know Christ in a real way."

She brushed aside my overtures. "No, he is going to be healed. I just know he is going to be healed." I marveled at her faith. Nothing could shake it. No words of mine, no medical prognosis could make a dent in her absolute assurance that he would be totally healed.

Finally, however, he died. Her reaction was immediate and violent. She hurled her Bible across the room. The postponement had not been granted. "If that's the kind of God you are," she shouted, "I want nothing to do with you!" At the funeral service she was barely civil to me and I felt the keen edge of her anger long after the service was over. God had not kept His part of the bargain, and since I was His only visible agent at the time, she let it be known she was through with God. To my knowledge she has not entered a church since. She was more violent than most in her reactions, yet it appears that charismatics are often prone to the same dangerous plea-bargaining with the Almighty, particularly in the area of healing.

No Thanatology (Doctrine of Death)

Since this theology stresses health, wealth, and prosperity almost exclusively, it has no real doctrine of death. One could fervently wish that they were right, and life held out promise of unlimited health, increasing wealth and continuous prosperity. Unfortunately, the harsh realities of death are still very much with us. Barring the Lord's return, while we are in these mortal bodies there is no escape from the last enemy. When people are conditioned to expect only health, there is little preparation for death. The apostle reminds us that we still groan in these mortal bodies awaiting redemption, but when the expectancy for life is too high, the dimension of death is unthinkable. Death is an unforgivable contradiction for anyone expecting perfect health, because between perfect health and death there is usually sickness, and sickness can never be of God. When death does come, the question is, "Who let them die?" The question is logical enough. Since health is in our hands through faith, when someone dies, the question calls for an answer. Someone is at fault.

Nowhere have we reaped the devastating consequences of this teaching more than in our own church. A number of people left our church confessing it was due to Martha's death. I recall very well the splendid young couple who were dedicated completely to serving the Lord. Their faith was simple and their trust was implicit; after Martha died, they left the church.

Bill approached them as to why. They answered truthfully, "Because, Bill, after Martha died we could no longer bear to see you." The problem for them was obvious. If Bill had exercised the proper faith, death would not have come. Reflecting on this incident, Bill said, "You know, I am convinced a charismatic church can handle divorce better than death."

On another occasion, a lady invited one of our fine ladies in the church to meet her for a late breakfast at Furr's

Cafeteria. She came with a mission of love and encouragement about a family situation. Although she had come previously to minister to Mary, the conversation finally got around to Bill and Martha. "But, Mary, Bill let Martha die."

"Let Martha die? What do you mean?"

"You know, he had her buried a little while after they found out she had cancer."

"That's not true. He has never buried her yet. He knows Marty is with the Lord."

Her friend looked at Mary. "Can I talk to you candidly? May I share with you some spiritual wisdom?"

"But of course," Mary responded. "I am always open to the insights of God's Word. Let me tell you that I am a believer in the Lord's healing power. In fact, I believed up to the day that she died. If the Lord let Martha die because of Bill's lack of faith, which by the way is not true, then why did my faith not cause her to live? My God does not allow any person to live or die because of my faith, or lack of faith. My faith is not in whether a person lives or dies, but in Jesus Christ alone."

No matter how well-intentioned it may be, no theology without an adequate view of death is complete. Apart from the charges of crypto-Christian Scientism, such a theology simply does not prepare its people adequately for the final exit. Normally, sickness of some kind is the passageway to that exit. The problem of dying is difficult enough as it is without complicating it further by heaping unjust condemnation on those who haven't "exercised faith" during the terminal stages God uses to bring most saints home. At the time when people need the greatest comfort and the most compassionate understanding, well-intentioned friends can be the agents of Satan to bring doubt and gloom and condemnation to the dying person.

The Bible brings the most comprehensive view of any philosophy or religion in the world to the question of death. Jesus acknowledged that death was real (John 11:14) but not final (John 11:25). He holds the keys of hell and death (Rev. 1:18). He has tasted death for every man (Heb. 2:9), and He delivers men from the second death in the here and now (John 5:24). For the Christian, death is the necessary enemy that must be faced before eternal felicity comes with his resurrected Lord. To focus on this life only and health in the here and now forfeits a balanced view of the whole counsel of God that recognizes death for the distasteful enemy it is, while setting its sights beyond to the great and really real world where "Eyes have not seen, nor ears beheld the glory God has prepared for those that love Him."

Works Righteousness

Gone is the persecution. Gone are the insults, railings, and accusations because one is called by that Name. Gone is the invitation to suffering and pilgrimage. Gone is the sweat, blood and tears of sacrifice that have been the distinguishing marks of great Christians through the centuries.

Instead, the very accoutrements of power and riches and material possessions against which earlier Christians have railed, from James, the brother of Jesus, to St. Francis of Assisi, have become the signs of the new righteousness gained by an exercise of faith. What man, in fact, in his carnal mind, would not choose this new gospel in preference to the old? The question left unanswered, however, is which gospel more approximates the actual life and deeds of Jesus of Nazareth. For those who want to live like King's kids, why settle for second best? Why not live like the King himself in the days of His flesh? Why not follow that walking, weary man of sorrows throughout His dusty homeland and sleep under the stars at night for the simple reason that not only at His birth, but for His whole life long, there continued to be "no room at the inn."

It is not a question of being saved by works; on that question all the writers stand in a solid reformation stream. They all agree we are saved by grace through faith in the finished work of the Lord Jesus. Salvation is a grace gift from the Lord.

The problem arises after salvation. Since all Christians have faith, and since faith is the sole factor in healing, it is an exercise of what I already have that heals me. The conclusion is obvious: if I am not healed, it is my fault. I have simply not exercised my faith. Just as there are physical exercises that will develop the body, and mental exercises to develop the mind, the same is true in the spiritual realm. I am saved by grace, but I am healed by working my faith. It is entirely up to me. If I need money, I also exercise faith. If I need prosperity, I must exercise faith. And eventually that faith will work, not sometimes, not 50 percent of the time, but all the time. It is clear then that prosperity and health are the new signs of the successful Christian. One's righteousness now is evidenced by his works of faith.

The apostle Paul, who boasted of his weakness, who

claimed that God had made the apostles laughingstock, like men condemned to die in the circus, who boasted in his humiliation, who confessed to being the scum of the earth, could only be judged by this theology as a foolish, unsuccessful Christian: he had failed to exercise his faith.

Gone completely is the great biblical doctrine of evangelical poverty. Gone is the emphasis on those who give up all to follow Him. Gone is the mentality that commands the rich young ruler to sell all he has, to give it away, and then to come and follow the Master. Gone is the call to cross-bearing and burden-sharing.

Kingdom Realized

One of the most persistent problems of theology has always been the mystery of the kingdom. What was the kingdom? When did it come, or has it? Is it in process of realization? Is it past? Is it future? Is it both? Much evangelical theology has perceived the kingdom as both present and future, in the here and now, and yet . . . not yet. As the King came once and will again return, so the kingdom came and will yet come. Where the King is, there is the kingdom. "The kingdom is among you." But the future brims with hope, for the suffering Messiah returns as the King of glory.

In this theology, however, there is a strong teaching that in essence the kingdom has already been realized. It is already come. It has already been provided. Health, wealth, prosperity and success. You name it, it's yours. You have kingdom rights. The secret abides in the exercise of faith. The kingdom is here and now, so get on with the program. "What you say is what you get," but a serious theological problem arises

If the kingdom has been realized, then what of death? There is no death in the kingdom. There are no tears, no crying, no thirst, and no scorching heat (Rev. 7:16). Death cannot live where there is only life. The King is life, so beside Him and with Him there is no death. It is obvious then that the kingdom has not, in fact, been yet fully realized We still live in our "terrestrial bodies"; we still bear "the image of the man of dust," and it is only in the future that "we shall also bear the image of the man of heaven" (1 Cor. 15:40-49).

We cannot do better than to review the words of Oswald Chambers:

Continually restate to yourself what the purpose of your life is. The destined end of man is not happiness, nor health, but holiness. The one thing that matters is whether man will accept the God who will make him holy. At all costs, a man must be related to God. (*My Utmost For His Highest*, p. 245)

8

Marty's Death

Cancer! I suppose that word strikes terror to the hearts of most people. It poses a special challenge to the Spirit-filled community, because so few people, comparatively speaking, are completely healed of this deadly killer. When it finally takes its toll, the Christian often faces another question. What happened? What went wrong? Whose faith failed? Who didn't fulfill his part of the bargain? Because their expectancy level is less, the problem is actually less severe for Christians who believe miracles ceased in the first few centuries; for those who consider the book of Acts as normative for experience as the epistles are for teaching, special problems exist.

A proper exegesis of Isaiah 53 and numerous New Testament passages leads to the inevitable conclusion that the early Church understood that Christ bore our sicknesses in the same way He bore our sins at Calvary. To the Christian for whom healing is a present day expectation, two courses of thought are possible when one is not healed.

One can simply argue from the sheer logic of the case. God entered into a contract with us and just as Christ has forgiven us our sins so He now heals us of our diseases. Since faith is the means by which our salvation is secured, faith is also the means whereby we are healed. Healing is simply an execution of faith according to the Word of God. Since the failure cannot be on God's part, when people are not healed, it must be our fault. There is only one answer, then, to a failure to receive healing—lack of faith. This position, with its Scripture and its logic, is extremely attractive to people who are searching. It appears to answer all questions of unexplained and unwanted deaths with one pat answer—lack of faith.

Another view says, "Not so fast! Although healing is in the Atonement, is it not possible that all the facts are not in? After all, even in the New Testament, not all sicknesses were healed. Paul, the great miracle worker, left Trophimus at Miletus sick (2 Tim. 4:20). He could not heal him. Undoubtedly they had prayed fervently, but for some reason God did not heal Trophimus. Paul himself suffered from a disease so loathsome that it could well have turned off his hearers just to see him (Gal. 4:13-15). He tells us he prayed long and hard for this disturbing interruption to disappear, but it did not. God gave him grace to bear it, and his illness became the occasion for the Galatians hearing the gospel.

Furthermore, a messenger from Satan troubled him so excessively he besought the Lord at least three times to take it away (2 Cor. 12:7-8). Paul enjoined Timothy to take wine for the health of his stomach (1 Tim. 5:23). Luke, the faithful physician, doubtless ministered to Paul's physical needs as he traveled all over Asia Minor with him. This view asks the question, have we considered sufficiently the sovereignty of God? Is it not possible that God permits sickness and calls some people home before the biblical "three score years and ten"?

I am convinced this was the case with Marty Sanders, beloved wife of our pastor, Bill. When a man becomes your buddy in warfare, suddenly his death—or the death of his loved one—is not just one more statistic that appears on the daily roll of fallen men, but such a death becomes a partial death for you. You find yourself, too, dying a little. John Donne, writing in a similar vein, said, "Never send to know for whom the bell tolls. It tolls for thee." All your philosophy about war in general being hell goes out the window and suddenly it is a particular hell—your particular hell. And the perspective inside of hell is quite different from philosophical speculation about its general disadvantages from the outside! That was the way I felt about Marty's passing, a good soldier had fallen along the way. My mind goes scudding back across the gentle years that Jo Ann and I, Bill and Marty, spent together as co-workers.

Several years previously God had called Bill and me to work in a special, spiritual partnership in the gospel. Our wives had rapidly become best friends. We grew together in the work of the Lord and became one team. We prayed together, we planned together, we traveled together to Israel on our yearly tours and our paths seemed to cross at every turn. Mondays were a special time when the four of us would go for lunch and prayer for people in the church. I remember the evenings with hamburgers and games in Bill's back yard, the fun times at the lake with our families and the picnics involving another family or two.

When in August of 1976 Marty rediscovered some nodes in her neck, it was a shock to all of us. She had made, it seemed, a complete recovery from her radical mastectomy of October, 1974, and no one anticipated more trouble.

Now Marty faced a choice: either to go the route of chemotherapy with its consequent problems of pain, loss of hair, sleeplessness and change in skin color, or to attempt to control the cancer through dietary means. As the decision was being formulated, a lady from the church put a challenging book into her hands. It was entitled *How I Conquered Cancer Naturally* by Edie May. It highly recommended Ann Wigmore's treatment center, Hippocrates' Health Institute in Boston, Massachusetts.

Many of us who had been bathing Marty in prayer, prayed in a special way that God would give His special wisdom from above. At that time I was far from sure of the merits of proper nutrition in the cure or control of cancer. To me, chemotherapy was a treatment of last resort. It spoke of delaying tactics at a price—untold suffering—and a few cures. I knew it eased the pain in some cases, but most of the nurses I knew who had seen others undergo the slow torture of chemotherapy were negative on its merits. A number had been outspoken.

"I simply would not have chemotherapy!"

"Chemotherapy is something physicians are particularly fond of, but from what I've seen, I couldn't advise it." These words from nurses did not encourage us.

What were they to do? Go the route of medical science or nutrition? At that point in time it seemed that all over the body of Christ in America there was a great new interest in nutrition. A spate of new information was available. People were claiming miraculous cures from the use of laetrile. New books and articles were almost weekly coming to our attention concerning the merits of this or that dietary path, and it simply seemed at that time that the nutritional route was the passage the Lord was indicating. When Bill and Martha decided to go this route, Jo Ann and I echoed a hearty amen. I fully expected the same wonderful results that had worked for Edie May and others. It was young David slaying Goliath all over again. The mighty giant, medicine, would have to bow to a righteous diet. I viewed the general disinterest of the medical community in a proper diet as evidence of medical arrogance; or even worse, the result of a monetary consideration. A physician once confessed to me, "There's no money in nutrition."

Now that it is over, I have had some time to reconsider. It is being generally accepted that nutrition is one of the keys to good health, but it is very far from a cure-all. On the other hand, the medical community seemed incredibly obtuse in the assumption that "American diets are just fine." I can remember on more than one occasion Jo Ann steaming home after her regular check-ups during a pregnancy.

"Oh, that doctor!"

"What's wrong, honey?"

"He didn't even check my diet, and he told me it was just fine."

"What did he ask?"

"All he wanted to know is whether I was eating enough. He didn't seem to care whether it was Rice Krispies or peanut butter sandwiches with marshmallows for dessert!"

I imagined a manufacturer buying a million-dollar gas engine equipped with the latest devices for his business. If the machine broke down, it seemed obvious to me that one of the first things he would check would be the quality of fuel.

"Here I am," I thought, "with an incredibly complex and irreplaceable machine, my body, and the expert never checks on the fuel intake. It just doesn't make sense."

On the other hand, I was equally convinced that the nutritionists had oversold their ideas by claiming too much too soon. One person is helped by a particular diet, and a book that is badly written and poorly documented suggests at least implicitly, if not explicitly, that if this particular diet were to be followed, a cure would inevitably ensue. Or, what is worse, someone writes yellow journalism, tying fantastic claims together with religious significance, sometimes with a sensational update on how this effects the Lord's return. In the process some genuinely helpful scientific technique is by-passed. Outlandish claims destroy the credibility of the genuine truth discovered and the scientific community passes over a good contribution. At times, the nutritionist movement births a publicity hound that makes all nutrition-conscious Americans sound as nutty as the fruitcake he is pandering.

Processes of true science demand an openness to truth from any quarter, and any scientist that dismisses herbs, plants and folk medicine is at that point simply being unscientific. The process of science itself demands that every viable answer be probed for its possible truth.

The fact that doctors consider medicine an art, not a science, does not absolve them of responsibility. Insofar as they are scientists, they need to consider proper nutrition as one of the ways God keeps us healthy. Furthermore, they need to reallocate some of the tremendous sums spent on a negative search for cures for illness into a positive search for good nutritional guidelines.

Science is like a ship, knowing generally where she is to go, but in the process of the journey she has to have all her planks, all her rails and every part of her structure, including the machinery, replaced while adjusting her direction to the new information continually available and all this without ever being able to put into harbor. It is like building a ship while she is sailing. When the process is working right, every hypothesis is being continually tested by the incoming evidence. Nutritional findings should be no exception.

At any rate, the value of a good diet was not lost on Marty. In September, 1976, she and Bill enrolled in the treatment center in Boston under Ann Wigmore's supervision. Marty followed an extremely strict diet composed mostly of wheat grass juice, sprouts and other organic things. I can remember thinking that no one in his right mind could stay on such a diet for very long. But Ann herself was the picture of perfect vitality and health. She never seemed to be tired and her "no nonsense" approach was practical and appealing. Bill and Marty took fresh hope. They returned from Boston filled with new expectations and everyone breathed a sigh of relief. The

Lord's word seemed to be in process of confirmation. He had assured me that Marty's illness was to be an educational experience for the whole church, and I understood that to mean that the whole body would learn new truths through a judicious use of the nutritional information that was coming to us through Marty's illness.

Marty stuck to her wheat grass juice diet with unbelievable fidelity. I have never seen a person exercise such discipline as far as diet was concerned. When the three of us were enjoying delicious food at our Monday luncheons, she stuck rigorously to her diet. Her discipline seemed justified. Her energy flow never ceased. She often remarked that she had never felt so well in her whole life.

Bill was equally faithful in growing the hard winter wheat for her juice. The stalks were grown in one to one-in-a-half inches of soil and when they reached a height of seven inches, they were cut and ground through a special machine. The awful-tasting result was wheat grass juice.

The days flew swiftly. Marty continued her jogging, but on March 30, 1977, she developed a bad cough that proved difficult to shake. On April 2, after considerable prayer, she entered Dr. H.A.A. Brown's Fairfield Medical Clinic in Montego Bay, Jamaica, accompanied by her attending physician and compassionate friend, Dr. Sybil Anderson. Dr. Brown held out high hopes for a complete cure. So many of his medical techniques fell into accord with what Marty was learning about nutrition, his optimism seemed justified. Although fully qualified as a physician, he used cobalt and chemotherapy only as a last resort. He preferred the use of vitamin supplements, including laetrile injections and tablets. He also used enzymes in tablet form.

Dr. Brown was a compassionate and optimistic doctor with a great concern for his patients. He assured Marty that many thousands of cancer patients in Germany and Europe were being cured by just such methods. Marty returned from Jamaica feeling great. She yielded up none of her activities and still enjoyed the out of doors. On May 4 she went picking strawberries and there received a muscle spasm. Dr. Roger Harmon, a Spirit-filled chiropractor in the church, eased her discomfort considerably. In early June she was still up to canning and freezing applesauce, but by mid-June, the toll was beginning to tell.

On June 13, she noticed considerable discomfort in the neck area. The tumors had never ceased growing despite the multiple injections she had received at Dr. Brown's clinic. Directly above her mastectomy on the right side, the tumors continued growing. Then new ones appeared on the left side of her neck and at length at the back of her neck. In the last stages, her left breast became as hard as a rock. The cancer had taken over.

The excruciating questions are obvious. If she had taken chemotherapy sooner, would she have lived longer? Her next-door neighbor, Jean, underwent extensive chemotherapy treatments. Her hair fell out, her skin grew yellow, but she has made a great comeback and has returned to work at the time of this writing. On the other hand, many people die within six months of the type of cancer Marty had.

Marty fought harder than any person I ever met. She simply would not slow down nor admit defeat. She continued to work from 7:00 A.M. until midnight taking care of the books and the many tasks that five children demand. June 17 was a particularly hard day for the family.

Finally, she said, "Honey, I am not getting any better. I am going downhill. Would you stay with me?" Bill did remain with her and they both came over to our house on June 20. She still looked beautiful, although tired. The next day, June 21, a rash started on her incision which became increasingly annoying. On June 22 she had difficulty swallowing her supplements and would start gagging as she tried to take them down. On June 27, she noticed how fast the tumors were growing. Bill expressed his agony, "Honey, it's not fair. It simply is not fair. We only have a few thousand praying for you."

She said, "Don't say that!"

He returned, "Why not?"

She answered, "Well, God knows what He is doing."

Bill went on, "I know it's not right to think this way, but if all the people who curse God, who smoke one cigarette after another, who don't eat what they should eat and give no credit to God live, then why should you not live?"

Their marriage had been a model marriage. They had enjoyed an unusually pure relationship before marriage. He had not held her hand until she knew she loved him and had not kissed her until shortly before the engagement. Bill often felt he could legitimately use his own marriage as an example of the gift God gives to all His children who put Him first in a holy and careful relationship before marriage. I remember reading a card a lovely lady in the church had sent him. It read: "Your family is the most beautiful family I have ever seen." Many in the church echoed those sentiments.

Marty never did ask why. Often when they were in prayer together, Marty would pray for wives who had husbands that were lost and would frequently weep over the tragedy befalling her friend, Jean, next door. She could weep for others, but Bill never heard her pray for herself. One day he stopped her. "Marty, you pray for everyone else, but I've never heard you pray for yourself."

She said, "But I do."

He rejoined, "I want to hear you." So she did.

Corrie ten Boom called twice.

"Marty."

"Yes, Tante Corrie."

"Marty, are you afraid to die?"

"No, Tante Corrie. I am not afraid to die, for I know that if I die, I'll be with Jesus."

But that wasn't the whole story. She really wanted to live; perhaps more than any other person I have ever met.

One day when she had returned to the hospital, Bill had quizzed her.

"I can think of a lot of reasons why I want to live."

Although her breathing was shallow and labored, she responded.

"I can, too."

"Oh," Bill baited, "and what are your reasons?"

She thought for a moment and gave four. "I'd like to be a better witness for the Lord, and, Bill, I'd really like to be a better wife to you."

He responded, "But, honey, you really are a nearly perfect wife."

She went on, "I also want to live for the children and

someday I'd love to see my grandchildren." She paused. "Then think what glory to the Lord the miracle of my healing would bring."

On July 5 and 6, Marty went to Dallas to see Dr. Brown, who was in town for a medical meeting. He urged her to return immediately to Jamaica for further treatment.

In many ways the three and a half weeks in Jamaica was a second honeymoon. Although Marty's treatments took most of the day, there were long hours of conversation, prayer and short walks around the lovely gardens. Bill had good exercise opportunities on the tennis court.

When Marty and Bill returned from Jamaica, only the family and a few others of us met them at the airport. Marty had to use a wheelchair, and that was when I almost gave up hope. I remember little Danny, their eleven-year-old son, pushing his mother. He was so protective and proud to help her, and she appeared so wan, frail and sick.

Marty had done her best to look chipper. A half smile played about her lips, but her neck was stiff with the pressure of the nodules. It made her head incline a little to the left.

"How are you doing, Marty?"

"Okay. I guess I'm a little tired."

But she wasn't okay. And I said as much to Jo Ann. "Honey, she just doesn't look good. She's so tired and weak. I'm sorry, but I don't think she's going to make it."

Marty never did regain her strength. She grew weaker daily. Finally on August 17 she was having such trouble breathing they took her to the hospital where they drained one and a half quarts of fluid from one lung. That lung never regained its use, so it was impossible to drain the other lung of its fluid. Only on her left side could she lay at all comfortably. During Marty's grim fight for life, the body of Christ joined in increasing prayer for a miracle. I have never really seen anything quite like it. The local body became the physical hands and feet of Christ. The prayers of the saints eased her pain and gentled her homegoing. Of that I am positive. Total strangers were drawn to strenuous prayer. Hundreds of churches and thousands of people joined hands around the world to pray for her recovery. No stone was left unturned as far as marshaling spiritual resources is concerned. Several of us unaccountably began to share empathetically in her symptoms of distress.

Nettie Hudson, one of our fine ladies in the church, couldn't breathe. She went outside fighting for air. "What is this, Lord?" She had no answer until later. Another woman had received a stiff neck and pains in the exact location of Marty's nodes. Still another had inexplicable pains in her lower back. Nothing seemed to be physically wrong. Tim Reside, our youth director at the time, had terrific stomach pains and all he could pray was, "Marty, Marty." And so it went. Each Sunday new people informed Barbara Primrose, our executive secretary at the Tulsa Christian Fellowship (T.C.F.) office, of special times at night when they were awakened from a sound sleep to intercede on her behalf. As I have analyzed stories that various members of the body related, only two factors appear constant: the vicarious sufferer was close to Marty and each one was known for the ministry of intercession.

Could this be what the apostle meant when he wrote to the Galatians, "My dear children, for whom I am again in the pains of childbirth until Christ is formed in you" (Gal. 4:19, NIV)? He gives us another hint, "[Even] now I rejoice in the midst of my sufferings on your behalf. And in my own person I am making up whatever is still lacking and remains to be completed [on our part] of Christ's afflictions, for the sake of His body, which is the Church" (Col. 1:24, TAB). Do intercessors have a part in the "full pale of Christ's afflictions yet to be endured"? Is this what Paul means when he says that when one member suffers, the whole body suffers?

My own experience occurred on a hot Tuesday in August. It was one of those humid days for which Tulsa is famous. They used to call them "dog days" back East. The air hung ominously quiet and still. Although it was early in the day, I knew it was going to be a scorcher. Jo Ann and I had prayed nearly unceasingly for Marty's recovery. We talked about little else.

On Tuesdays, my regular day of fasting and prayer, I prayed alone in my little study. The second name on my long list of people was Marty. I had barely uttered her name before a terrifying "something" hit me. I could not breathe. I felt as though someone had placed a hand over my nose and mouth and was deliberately permitting only sufficient air to pass through to keep me alive. I panicked. I could no longer kneel. I rushed out of the room. I began to pace restlessly back and forth, up and down, throughout the house. I wanted to run outside but the stifling air would only have complicated the problem. Still unable to breathe, I rushed to the church office where I had an appointment for counseling. I could hardly sit through the session. I don't remember a word that was said, but I remember praying, "Oh, Lord, please don't let me faint. It would be too embarrassing." After the lady left, Mary Ann, one of our church secretaries, came in. I told her about my problem. She mentioned that on the radio that morning she had heard that the heat had absorbed the ozone of the air making it difficult to breathe. Later I checked with my doctor, who didn't give much credence to the idea, but momentarily it gave me at least some rational explanation for my totally irrational behavior. I was panicked by my inability to get my breath.

I staggered on to my next appointment at the Living Sound office. Terry Law went over some business with me, but I found I was unable to concentrate. I kept fading in and out. His voice was clear and then would drift away. He was alarmed. "Chuck, let me take you home."

"Thanks, Terry, but that won't be necessary."

I remember lumbering out of the office. "Dear God," I prayed, "please help me to get home."

Nothing seemed to help. I found the coolest spot in the house and propped up my feet. My heart began to beat, faster and faster. My pulse began to pound. I called my good friend and compassionate colleague, Dr. Jim Krafft.

"Jim, I can't explain it. I'm not doing a thing but my heart is pounding like mad."

"Take your pulse."

"Okay." I did and reluctantly gave him some unbelievable figure.

"Chuck, come in right away for some heart tests. I'll see you there shortly."

I protested. "Jim, I know it's not my heart. I don't know what it is, but I simply can't get my breath."

"Come in anyhow."

I promised to be there, but by the time Jim had reached his office, his efficient staff had already completed the EKG test, and by a plug-in system with a local hospital, the entire read out came back immediately. Everything checked out perfectly. My heart was okay. Jim led me to his office. Then he looked me straight in the eye.

"Chuck, this is really in your ball park."

I took the words in slowly. Jim was saying there was a spiritual or emotional causation. There was nothing wrong physically. He went on.

"You can control your breathing. You can refuse to hyperventilate. It is in your power."

Still puzzled, but somewhat relieved, I returned home. At 5 o'clock on that blistering afternoon, Jo Ann, who had just returned from a visit to Martha, began to describe the difficulty she was having with breathing. Again the terror struck. I could not breathe.

"Stop it, honey. Don't say another word! I simply can't stand it." Again the massive hand seemed to choke off my air. It was simply impossible to get a decent breath. Even as I fought down the panic, an unshakable spiritual revelation came through as clear as a bell.

"This is for Martha. This is what she is going through. I don't see how she stands it!" That night in bed I quizzed Jo Ann about deep breathing.

"Honey, tell me about breathing from the diaphragm." I knew she had learned this technique for the birth of our youngest child, Melissa Hana, and through its use her delivery was an exuberant and joyous experience. She told me a little.

"Now teach me how."

"Out (diaphragm expands)—in (diaphragm retracts). Out—in—out—in—out—slow! Slow! Wait! Now out. Now in. Now out. Now in. Now out." Slowly I began to catch on and began to fall into the rhythm of the system.

The next day I visited Bill and Marty. Except for one brief moment, it was to be the last time I saw Marty alive. I remember explaining to her what I had experienced the day before. Bill sat nearby on the bed.

"Why," she said, "that checks out exactly with what I've been experiencing."

"Marty," I said, "let me teach you what Jo Ann taught me. In—out—in—out—in—out." A half-hour slowly ticked by. "In—out—in—out—in—out—in—out—in—out." When I left she seemed to be breathing easier. Later she remarked that without this breathing technique she wouldn't have made it.

While in the hospital, Dr. Sybil Anderson said to Bill, "We must get a pink room ready for Martha before she returns home. Pink is such a healing color." The idea took hold. At last there was something in a material way the church could do besides pray. Shirley Meeks and Ann Phillips made it a special love project of their own. Both are decorators; in an amazingly short period of time they were able to purchase matching curtains, bedspreads and sheets. Beautiful pictures filled the room. Two of the men of the church worked until the early hours of the morning to paint the room. As an old painter myself, I remember being concerned about any lingering paint fumes, but there was no problem. Someone found an elegant pink carpet and it was laid in record time. The room was beautiful and ready in a matter of twenty-four hours. Marty returned home to her special pink room.

I never met anyone with more tenacity to live. A couple of days before she died she asked, "Bill, have you given up?"

"No way, Marty, no way."

Then she paused and whispered, "And the people—have the people given up?"

"No, the people have not given up."

Another pause.

"Well, if they had, I would have given up, too."

Even though sleep had long since fled except for short catnaps, Marty refused all sleeping pills. It had always been that way. She had never wanted aspirin or anything else that might poison her system.

During Marty's rapid decline, the whole body of believers rallied in almost round-the-clock praying. The night before she died I prayed, "Lord, let the angels of peace and gentleness fill that pink room. Lord Jesus, please be gentle; be very, very gentle with her." The tears flooded my eyes. My words surprised me. I had never prayed that way before, but a deep peace settled over me as I sank into sleep.

During that last night Bill sat beside her alternately reading and dozing. She said, "Bill."

He responded, "Do you need anything?"

"No—I just wanted to make sure you were still there."

So it went through the long night. At 4:45 A.M. on Friday, August 26, Bill went to the kitchen for a few minutes, mixed some yogurt and bananas and returned to the bedroom.

"Honey, what are you eating?"

"Some yogurt and bananas."

"May I have some?"

"Of course, honey, please have some." Bill was elated. She hadn't really eaten in weeks. Then she promptly proceeded to polish off the whole bowl. A little later, "Honey, I'm going to have to get some rest. Maybe I'd better have a shot." Her breath was coming in brief, shallow pants. Oxygen was always at hand and had been used throughout the whole ordeal. Bill left for a few minutes to get some medication and do a few errands. Her daughter, Shirley, stayed to watch. Five minutes went by.

"Shirley, where is daddy?"

"He went out to get some medicine."

"Well, shouldn't he be back by now?"

Already the time sequence had blurred. At death, time and eternity seem to merge.

Bill returned, gave her the shot, but it was ineffective. She was simply groggy.

That morning Jo Ann had been wondering who should spend time with Marty, because she had volunteered to coordinate those who sat with her. The people selected had to be quiet, secure people who did not overtax or overtire Marty. I thought for a moment.

"Honey, today I think you'd better go over," I said. She leaped at the opportunity and so Jo Ann spent that last afternoon with Marty in her beautiful, newly decorated room while Bill tried to sleep. It was no use. Every five minutes Jo Ann came to the door, "Bill, Marty wants you." Later she explained that Marty didn't really want anyone but Bill to help her, no matter what it was. When Jo Ann returned that night, I was concerned.

"How did it go, honey? Was it terribly draining?" I thought of the horrible, labored breathing, Marty's discomfort in any position, the many demands a sick person must make and the disquieting knowledge that a loved one is slowly slipping away. Jo Ann hadn't been sleeping much herself and Marty was all she talked or thought about. She surprised me.

"Honey," she said, "it was really wonderful! That whole room is so full of peace. It was a great experience just being there. It was so quiet and restful, as though there were angels present."

During the day Bill followed a little ritual each time Marty called for him. He took her by the hands, lifted her up to a sitting position on the side of the bed, knelt in front of her, placed her feet on his attaché case and laid her head on his left shoulder. It was the only way she could be comfortable. She would rest a little while there and then be ready to lie down again. Then he would play his little game. He squeezed her hand three times. I love you. Then she tapped him three times in return.

"Honey," he said, "I'm sorry that shot didn't work. Do you want me to call Dr. Crawford?"

"Maybe you'd better."

The shot held her for three or four hours. About 8 o'clock that evening, Bill and the family were sitting around eating a late supper. Terror struck Bill in the pit of the stomach. He jumped up from the table, ran into the bedroom, knelt by her side and immediately noticed her tortured breathing.

"Honey, are you okay?"

She mumbled something unintelligible. He tried to raise

her up as he had done so many times before. This time she couldn't help. Bill put his right hand under her but only got her halfway up.

She said, "No, I can't make it. Put me down."

Her breathing grew heavier, louder, more tortured, then it stopped all together. She was gone.

"Honey, honey," he called. But there was no answer. He did not try to call her back.

A few minutes later I received a phone call. It was Bill. "My little girl has gone home," he said. "She is with Jesus."

I was stunned! What did the strange prayer of the night before mean? The prayer that came to my lips but did not originate with me? What did the quiet peace of the afternoon mean? Why had Jo Ann spoken of the angel messengers if they were not there to heal? Slowly the light dawned. The Spirit had led my prayer request of the night before and Jo Ann was the witness to its answer. The angels of peace had come, but not to heal. They had come to cradle her back to God.

As we rushed to Bill's house, I had the most loving experience with Jesus I had ever known. It was so excruciatingly painful and yet so exquisitely intimate that even when I write at this distance in time and space, the tears start. We sped toward Bill's house. Although I wept with racking sobs that left me gulping for air, and though the tears came cascading down in torrents so that I could scarcely see the road, my spirit soared toward Jesus in a love experience I've never had before or since. It was as though a great light had come and my spirit was rising with angelic beings toward ever increasing light. I knew. I knew. I knew as I had never known before. In that mystical moment of agony and ecstasy, my doubts about Christ really being touched by our human griefs and sorrows were burnt up as though consumed by a holy fire. Jesus really did care! I had heard it. Now I knew it. He had tenderness I had never before experienced. The farther my spirit traveled outwards the more compassion I felt. He had a compassion that beggars words. A new thought struck me. In the midst of excruciating pain, compassion was deepest.

Only one other time have I been so close to Christ. One night in a prayer meeting many years ago the air suddenly began to crackle and change. The atmosphere clouded over and I saw a great fog roll into the entire room. Suddenly I was being pierced by the eyes of Jesus Christ. They were the boldest, most challenging eyes I had ever seen. There was not a vestige of sympathy in them. I could not see any other features of His face clearly except those burning, unblinking eyes. His eyes bored into every nook and cranny of my being. I turned to Jo Ann, "Honey, do you see what I see?"

She responded, "I see something, but I don't know what it is." Then I turned back to face those eyes. They seemed to say, "Chuck, I challenge you to do more, to give more, to be more. I want all of you there is; you can do better." My eyes riveted to His and my spirit ascended. The moments merged into timelessness. For me eternity had entered time. "Lord, what I have is yours. All of it." Slowly the fog cleared. That was all, but I have never been able to erase that electrifying memory from my mind.

So when I encountered Christ in His compassion, a great swelling of gratitude surged through my spirit. "Thank you, Jesus. Thank you. You are so gentle, so kind. I love you, Jesus. I love you! I thank you that you didn't leave us down here all alone. You really *do* care." This was the first time I had ever experienced the unspeakable joy there is in the fellowship of suffering.

Bill called the children together and they wept for a while. Then Bill prayed, "Lord, you know how I loved to hold her and how she loved to be held. So you hear my prayer. She is now at your feet and in your presence; so I want you to take her in your arms and hold her real tight." He heard a distinct voice. At first he thought it was one of the children.

Don't you think I can do a better job than you did?

He turned to the children. "Which one of you said that?"

"Not I." "Not I." "Not I." None of them had spoken a word.

While Marty was slipping away, some ladies at an Episcopal retreat suddenly began to weep. Marty came to mind. They later understood why. A group of young people were on a youth retreat. The girls had separated themselves and the Lord told them that Marty had gone home. One lady had the vision of Marty holding a baby with a big smile on her face. She didn't know that Bill and Marty had lost a baby. Another lady saw her running in a field of flowers surrounded by joy and happiness. Marty had always loved flowers. Even her prayer to be a better witness was answered. Immediately after the funeral service a woman gave her life to Christ and a father rededicated his life in the pink room where Marty had died.

The funeral service was memorable. Unexpectedly, Bill

spoke for a good twenty minutes sharing with the congregation the innermost parts of his heart. I have never seen such raw, bleeding humanity exposed to brothers and sisters in the manner in which he opened himself up that day. It was as though he turned himself inside out and deliberately ferreted out each crack and corner of his heart, and, with a courage I have seldom seen equaled, appeared to be saying to one and all, "Here. Here I am! Sure it hurts. It hurts something fierce, but God is here. I've been to the bottom, and He is here. Here at the end of the journey. It's real, folks—what you heard of Christ's comfort is true."

I remember thinking, "Bill, you're going too far; you're saying too much. It's better to leave some things left unsaid." Embarrassed, I began to twist and turn. "Bill, please sit down," I thought.

But Bill went right on until he finished what he had to say. There were many weeping when he sat down.

I need not have worried about the congregation's response. Later on, when I guardedly inquired of an intellectual and dignified friend what he thought of the service, he said, "It was exactly what should have been." I was relieved.

There were other questions harder to handle. One obstinate and perplexing question that kept surfacing troubled many of Marty's friends. Who's to blame?

There seems to be something in us that is dissatisfied until it finds out the cause of all things. The philosophers have often remarked on this tendency in man. A tragedy has occurred; someone's to blame. No one really has the guts to blame God; someone must be guilty; so who's to blame? Theology is reviewed. Christ carried our sicknesses as well as our sins. How, then, can we account for this event called death? It seems to me that Spirit-filled Christians often resent being reminded that their last enemy has not yet been conquered; but death still prevails for saint as well as sinner. People still die, and we have to live with that frailty and that knowledge. It is as though the Spirit-filled community chooses to believe that the kingdom has already come; that we are already in the millennium, and if only we will think positively enough and recite the proper formulas loud enough, even death can be conquered. It is a tempting thought. Unfortunately, we still live within the confines of our time-space universe.

The question is not a new one. I have often reflected on the contemporaneity of history; its repetitiveness. The same things keep happening over and over again with different names, different times and different places, but the ingredients remain the same. I think it was Santayana who said, "Those who do not remember the past are condemned to repeat it." Fact is, whether we learn from history or not, we still repeat the same questions and give the same answers that were given centuries ago.

Most of the answers are no better than they were in Job's day. In Job's time the same witch hunt went on. Job's comforters, Eliphaz, Bildad, and Zophar, arrived on the scene from different parts of the Middle East. They came to sympathize with him, they came to comfort him. Some sympathy, some comfort! Poor Job!

God permitted Satan to try him on a single day to an extent no other man has ever experienced. He lost 7,000 sheep, 3,000 camels, 500 female donkeys, and worst of all, seven sons and three daughters, in a single day. After all this trouble, the comforters arrive and begin to heap their theology on him. Clarity, if not truth, distinguishes their argument. "The truth remains that if you do not prosper, it is because you are wicked. And your bright flame shall be put out" (Job 18:5, TLB).

In other words, their theology had it all together, their syllogism was simple and sounded correct.

Major premise: God rewards the righteous and punishes the wicked.

Minor premise: Job is being punished. (No one could deny that fact!)

Conclusion: Therefore, Job cannot be righteous.

All through the book they make their point, again and again, as they dream up fanciful facts to prove it. They accuse him of adultery, of robbing widows and orphans, of defaulting people of their rightful due and of indulging in every kind of wickedness man is capable of doing.

Job protests in vain. He has not done any of the things his accusers heap on top of his head, and it's hard to tell from the text whether the suffering from the boils or the comfort of his friends causes the worst pain. His friends refuse to believe him. The fact that they had no facts to support their case didn't stop them a bit. Like many a modern theologian, the plain facts of the case didn't in any way interrupt the flow of their theology. When the facts did not fit the case, like Procrustes they just simply stretched the facts to fit their ideas. It was clear Job was suffering; therefore, he had to be unrighteous. No other possibility entered their thinking.

I often tell my theology students, "If your theology doesn't fit the facts, change your theology." That doesn't seem to be a great piece of revelation or a particularly magnificent formulation of intellectual endeavor, but it is surprising to see how difficult it is to get people to change a fixed idea.

A beautiful miracle happens right in front of their eyes, and what do they say? "I don't believe it. Miracles don't happen today!" In fact, sometimes unbelievers appear to believe more than the believers. Too often the attitude of people is, "My mind is made up; please don't confuse me with the facts." But we must remember how God dealt with them in the end. It's always good to find out how matters end. There, God justified Job rather than his friends. God told them He was angry because they had not spoken what was right concerning Him. Furthermore, they were to bring seven bullocks and seven rams to Job who would offer them to God. When he prayed, "the Lord accepted Job's prayer" (Job 42:7-9).

"What a humiliating experience!" they thought. "Here we have been defending God all this time and what He is doing now is not fair. He's telling us we are wrong. He is saying our theology is off, and to make it even worse, he makes us go to this wicked man, Job, in order to receive forgiveness."

I wonder if sometimes in the past I may not have been guilty of counseling as Job's comforters did, and if I had heard directly from God, He might not have said the same thing to me.

Someone has written a little paragraph that tells it graphically.

CAESAREA PHILIPPI (If Peter had been a theologian.)

There is a story going around here which purports to update the 2,000-year-old report of Matthew, in order to make it more relevant to the current ascendancy of theology as the basis of religious belief. Report of Matthew's account has received the following revision: "When Jesus came to the neighborhood of Caesarea (Philippi) He asked His disciples this question: 'Who do people say the Son of Man is?' They replied, 'Some say John the Baptizer, others Elijah, still others, Jeremiah or one of the prophets.' 'And you,' He said to them, 'who do you say that I am?' Simon Peter answered, 'You are the eschatological manifestation of the ground of being and of the faith community, the *kerygma* manifested in conflict, the self-realization of personhood and the motivational encounter for the process of humanizing and socializing mankind.' And Jesus replied, 'I'm what?' Then He strictly ordered His disciples not to tell anyone who He was, for He found that He could not recall the formula and repeat it Himself. (*The Courier,* Milwaukee, August 17, 1973, p. 1)

There is something in us that demands an answer to our whys. Perhaps it is part of our fallenness from God to question every tragedy, demanding it to yield an answer to us in the same way Eve demanded the knowledge of good and evil. A child is struck down; the first question, "Why?" Cancer strikes a Christian, "Why?" What sin did he commit? A man is electrocuted; again, "Why?" It seems that nineteen centuries of our Lord's teaching about the essential mystery of tragedy has hardly penetrated our hearts and minds at all (John 9). We are so ruled by intellect that I have often wondered if knowledge is not the devil's substitute for faith. We would rather know why than trust the Father. We would rather have an answer to our questions than solutions to our problems. I have always been intrigued by the bishop in C.S. Lewis's book, *The Great Divorce*, who, when offered heaven, preferred a discussion group in hell.

Job's comforters keep reappearing in every generation with their particular solution to an essentially insoluble mystery. In Martha's case it was the same. Enter Zophar, Bildad, and Eliphaz. If there is a tragedy, there must be a reason, and the tacit unspoken corollary follows that if there is a reason we should be able to search it out. For example, there was the reason of wrong doctrine. Before Martha died one woman expressed a generally held position to one of Tulsa Christian Fellowship's members, "Your church is not hearing the right kind of doctrine. I feel impelled to warn you that Martha is going to die. T.C.F. doesn't teach the faith message. You had better get out while you can. T.C.F. is not worth dying for."

Others, like Job's comforters, held that it was our sins that explained Martha's illness. One woman asked for an audience with the elders and staff. "Martha's cancer is related to the sin in T.C.F. There is a man here you haven't forgiven, and this is eating away at all of you. The cancer in Martha's body exists because you have not exercised a forgiving spirit."

The elders sat quietly through the explanation and accusation. Afterwards, each one indicated that to the best of his knowledge, he had indeed forgiven the man in question. The elders later came to the consensus that this was another attempt by the enemy to bring condemnation into the body in an experience that could ultimately shatter faith.

The woman went on. "Yes, Martha is being sacrificed; sacrificed for the sins of T.C.F. She is dying for those sins."

An elder objected, "But Jesus was the one and only perfect sacrifice for our sins. His was enough."

Guilt is an easy product to sell in the midst of an inexplicable death. The offices of counselors and psychiatrists bulge to overflowing with people who have guilt flowing out their ears. The problem is not to make people feel guilty; the problem is to deliver them from condemnation.

Another explanation was the partial gospel theory. One woman spoke to this problem as she perceived it.

"Martha is dying because the pastors are preaching a watered-down gospel. They do not really preach faith there and, therefore, you have to get out of T.C.F. in order to hear the truth. In fact," she volunteered, "I have an idea. Let's start a prayer meeting here in your home where we can bring in outside preachers and teachers that really teach the truth about faith."

A lady pointed to the burgeoning numbers attending a church preaching a "strong faith" message as proof positive that God's blessing rested on that message.

"T.C.F. is full of doubt and unbelief," she said. "Martha died because of the lack of faith. God did not will Martha's death in this way. She did not need to die."

On the other hand, Martha's passing only increased the quagmire of guilt for others. One troubled husband bared his heart to his wife. "Honey, I don't want to return to church. Martha Sanders was the most holy woman I knew, and if the Lord let her die, then there is no chance for a sinner like me."

Others took a different tack. One diffident and shy young man who had never prophesied before stood before a group of thirty-five people with joy and great elation. God had given him a message that he had interpreted to mean that Martha would be healed. In the midst of Bill's message one Sunday, God had told him Bill would not be left alone. He understood this to mean Martha's healing. It did not occur to him that God's comfort could be the companion for Bill during the hard months following Martha's death, as was in fact the case. Or that it may have been the promise of a future partner.

On the brighter side of the ledger, there were beautiful visions that reflected Martha's homegoing. A group of six people gathered socially when a strong spirit of intercession suddenly swept over them. They prayed for Martha, and as they did, one of the ladies saw Jesus go to her bed, gather her in His arms and kiss her. He held her gently for a long time, then walked away with her cradled in His arms.

Another saw Martha before Jesus in a weak, crumpled heap, utterly unable to raise even her face to Him. In His purple robes, Jesus walked over to her and gave her a white rose.

"This is for purity," He said. After handing her the rose, He stooped down, took her hand and said, "Arise, my daughter, and be made whole." Then He walked away, holding her by the hand. This was on the Thursday night before she died.

The week before Martha entered the hospital, different members of the body expressed a strange inclination to relinquish her to the Lord, but felt guilty about this type of surrender as though it were a kind of betrayal. People did not dare to voice their doubts about recovery. Everyone was being constantly challenged to exercise faith. However, an inner surrender of Marty began simultaneously in various parts of the body. Questions unshared, not to be spoken of, a hushed matter, but nonetheless there. People were torn between what they felt in their hearts and what they felt obliged to confess with their lips.

One young wife saw herself carrying Martha into the throne room where she was on her knees and the Lord reached down and picked up Martha, held her, and hugged her in such a way that His great love for her was very evident. She began to cry, and then motioned to God to give Martha back. The Lord did not respond. He continued to hold her, and as she was trying to explain to God, "They are all waiting, I have to bring her back," she was forced to leave her in God's arms, just holding her.

The young woman was unable to understand the incident, because she felt it wasn't right to dampen the Spirit, or prayers for her healing. In a couple of weeks, Martha went home. The vision's authenticity was confirmed to her.

Probably one of the most comforting dreams occurred to Alma Lou, one of the fine ladies of the church, a few days before Thanksgiving. In her dream, Martha was standing before her, radiant and beautiful, and Alma Lou exclaimed, "Marty, what are you doing here?"

"I was given permission to be with my family for a while and since I was on my way back, I thought I would drop by to see you." She began to smile and it was like a warm embrace from the Father.

"Marty—I have so many questions to ask. Are you allowed to answer them?"

She responded, "Sure, what do you want to know?"

"My first question is, have you seen my father yet? I know there are so many people to see and meet."

"I guess not, Alma Lou. What is his name?"

"Clifford James. Here, let me write it down for you so you won't forget it." And she whirled around to write her father's name on the corner of an envelope. She handed it to Marty. She put out her hand gently but pushed it back and said, "I won't need that. I'll remember his name. Besides, that paper would only disintegrate by the time I get back."

"Do you eat in heaven?"

"You know how I love fruit, Alma Lou. I just go to a tree, pluck its food and eat it. It's really delicious, and there is no waste, no core to throw away. And, there is no digestion process so we have no waste in us either."

Her third question followed. "Marty, what is it like to see the Master?" At this point Marty's face took on a particular glow and her eyes changed to become almost those of Jesus himself as she answered, "Alma Lou, there are no earthly words that can describe our Master." Her voice was soft and reverent, and her face glowed to match her words.

Then she asked, "Marty, do you know what goes on down here?" Martha gave an indirect answer. "Oh, Alma Lou, we intercede all the time." The dream faded.

When the formulas don't work, they drive us away from God. Over the past months I have spoken to a number of people who have almost totally lost faith because the formulas they had been given by some teacher didn't work out according to their confession.

Just the other day I was chatting with a lovely young mother who had almost settled into cynicism and despair because the formulas she had tried didn't work. Her reasoning was sound enough.

"I have tried the formulas and they didn't work. Either God is wrong or I am wrong. Since God cannot be wrong, there must be something terribly wrong with me. If I can't believe God here and in this crisis, how can I believe Him for anything else?" In her own words she had just about lost all faith.

Fortunately, about that time, she heard a teaching which helped to rescue her from the quagmire of her own logic. The teaching stressed the sovereignty of God and the dangers of presumption. It comforted her heart with the assurance of God's compassion and overwhelming love in situations we do not understand.

Not all, however, are so fortunate. The other day I was chatting with a friend who told me a very remarkable exchange he had seen occur at a table where he was eating with one of the teachers of this doctrine. A splendid, well-dressed, young businessman approached the table.

"Please," he said, "may I ask you a question? I am

really sold on everything you teach about confession bringing possession. I believe God wants me to prosper; in fact, I bought all seventy of your tapes and over a six-month period heard them over and over again. I did exactly what you said. I exercised my faith, and launched out into a business venture, but in six months I went totally bankrupt. I tried everything I knew. Please tell me. What did I do wrong?''

The teacher grew red-faced and defensive. He bristled, ''But it has to work! It simply has to work!'' That was his only answer.

I can't help wondering what happened to that young man. Did he wander away bewildered and lost because there were no better answers?

To get people's minds released from certain formulas they have learned, and back on to the Lord himself, is one of the most difficult pastoral tasks I have. Sometimes, it sounds like a broken record. ''God has said it, so I must believe it, and He will do it.'' Often in the early days of the prayer groups after we had finished praying for some seriously ill person, someone would inevitably say, ''Now you are healed, just claim it and praise the Lord for your healing. Any pain that remains is only a lying symptom.'' I used to cringe inside when some of them grew worse and others even died. I always found the answer ''But they simply didn't exercise faith'' too glib and superficial. As Jamie Buckingham said, ''Much of what we call faith is merely irreverent brashness. Healing, like joy, does not come from God's promises, but from His presence. It does not depend upon our faith, but upon His mercy'' (*The Trumpet*, May 3, 1978).

The clichés were either hypocritical or an irresponsible flight from reality. I began to wonder, "Don't these people feel any sense of responsibility for the words they utter? They speak about a positive confession. What about words of certainty to people for whom it does not work? Don't they care about what happens to their faith? How can they be so cocksure all these people have no faith?"

The Goodness of God in Tragedy

God is love in disappointment as well as success. God's compassion and love are perhaps even more apparent in the starkest tragedy than in the greatest joy. One of the striking similarities in the visions and dreams people had surrounding Marty's death was the loving and particularized attention God paid to her. He, himself, held her like a little child. He had seemed in some of the visions to be reluctant to let her go. He had cherished her just as she had been cherished below. To the intellectually sophisticated, I suspect all the visions people reported could be explained away as naive wish fulfillments. To be truthful, I gave some thought to the problem the recounting of visions might create for some of my intellectual friends. The argument could go that visions are no more than the unconscious projections of the way people wished things were. Critics might argue that visions are no more than projections of the human soul representing the mind's attempt to heal the organism of its grief. It is a self-healing mechanism within the person himself

But to argue in this fashion is to belie the biblical tradition. Visions and dreams receive solid biblical support; they form the basis of a good deal of our eschatology and furnish all Christians with a theology of hope. Daniel and Revelation—both the results of visions—reflect a single theme: God wins in the end. It does not seem surprising that God should still use dreams and visions to comfort His people. After all, this activity is no more than a fulfillment of Peter's first sermon. He said in essence, "The last days have come, the new age has dawned, and it is a fulfillment of Joel's prophecy when the Spirit is poured out on all flesh. Your sons and daughters shall prophesy and your youth shall see visions; your elders shall dream dreams."

As long as we do not rely on visions or prophecy for new doctrine, and as long as they conform to the overall witness of Scripture, they can be great comforters and attesters to the goodness of God in time of sorrow.

I reflected back on my own freeway experience as Jo Ann and I sped along to comfort Bill at the time of Martha's death. I could no more deny the reality of that experience than Pascal could deny the half-hour of ecstasy he enjoyed which drenched him so overwhelmingly in the liquid fire of divine love, that he had to ask God to hold it back. It transformed him into one of the great Christian apologists of all time. The heightened reality of those few moments on the freeway was really an authentic encounter for me with eternity, in which the pain of the loss and the realization of Christ's compassion brought me so close to ultimate reality that I do not know to this day if I wept harder at the loss or was dissolved to tears by the love. But no one could persuade me that I had fled from reality. It would be more accurate to say I had been drawn into a greater reality. C.S. Lewis pictures heaven as the place where things are really *real*, and evil walks around like ghostly ghouls and shadows.

Since life is a learning process and nothing educates us so fast in life as death, what conclusions could be drawn? Probably the first thing I learned is that there are no easy answers. The easy answers turned out to be no answers at all. The reasons people gave for Marty's passing seemed not so much to be frivolous as they were irrelevant. They simply did not speak to the real issues even when the answers would have been true in some cases; they did not ring true here. Marty's death did not occur because there was no faith exercised, or the elders were involved in some great sin, or the church taught the wrong doctrine, or the doctors were consulted too late, or the nutritionists were unskilled. Each of these questions had at some time or other been squarely faced and answered.

But after a barrage of different answers appeared, I asked myself, "Why are people so intent on giving answers? Why do they have this inner compulsion to explain the tragic mysteries?" Although people meant well, I considered some of the bizarre and even cruel answers good people gave and I began to gain a new insight into human behavior.

Everyone wants a scapegoat. When something goes wrong, there needs to be someone or something to blame. When an adequate scapegoat fails to materialize, people become frustrated. For many, better a tentative or wrong answer than no answer at all. Somehow, even when we don't really know the whys and wherefores, it seems to set our minds at ease to think we have the reasons.

In some ways this experience was a backward step in

knowing, but a forward step in growing. Long ago someone said, "Growth in grace is not growth in knowledge but growth in dependence." That certainly held true for me. God's perspective came into clearer focus than ever before. It was as though all His encouragements and consolations amounted to His saying, "No big deal! Death may be a giant barrier down there, but it is a small step to over here. It was all in my timing, and Marty would not return if she could."

There are mistakes or sins Christians commit that take them home early. Paul comments on this to the Corinthian church, where Christians died prematurely due to taking the Lord's Supper without due respect (1 Cor. 11:29-30). Christians also die before their time from improper nourishment and neglect of the body, but I am quite confident Marty went home at the proper time in the sovereignty of God and there I am quite content to rest.

9

New Testament Church: Larva or Adult?

It has been the thesis of this book that there is a real distinction between faith and presumption; that much of what passes for faith today is in fact presumption. Failure to distinguish the difference between these two has caused untold anguish to thousands of sincere and dedicated Spirit-filled Christians for whom the ordinary formulas have not worked. My purpose, therefore, is to reassert the doctrine of the sovereignty of God to an age of Christians who have felt that somehow it is now up to them; to point people back to the living God himself, not to principles about God however valid they may be. The discovery and application of certain formulas appears to be the purpose of most of the "faith" teachers.

A further question, however, remains for those who have embarked on the raft of "risky living," which Jamie Buckingham advocates. Experienced beyond what traditional Christianity offers and yet uncomfortable with much of present charismatic teaching with its simplistic answers, what help is there for the thinking Christian who desires a sane spiritual balance without sacrificing the new powers and gifts the Holy Spirit is presently bringing? Is there a way out of the present dilemma? Since we have become pilgrims in a larger place, how can we formulate our new understandings in such a way that they are true both to our experience of Christ and the Scriptures? This is the task of theology.

I believe there is a way and that it can be succinctly stated in a simple proposition: *The New Testament furnishes us with principles of a pattern church that can and should be followed today.*

If one holds this to be true he must believe that the New Testament Church emerges as a model of church life which is safe to follow. In the New Testament we find not only the pattern of the Spirit's power and gifts, but also the forms and structures of the Church which should be emulated today. In renewal circles this is known as the restoration movement.

Yet to tread this path is to walk into the middle of a theological hailstorm. Very few theologians will buy the premise of this chapter; the New Testament furnishes not only the doctrinal norms but also the pattern forms for church life. A great controversy rages concerning the New Testament Church. Do we have here an embryo, an undeveloped but lively experience in the early life of the Church that was meant to pass away? Or do we have here a model, a pattern safe for all succeeding generations of Christians to follow, duly interpreted from within their own culture in space and time? Was the New Testament

Church meant to furnish us mainly with the authoritative apostolic teachings or was it meant to have some particular instructions for us in structure? Does the New Testament give us form as well as content? In short, what do we have in the New Testament: larva or adult?

It is my understanding that the book of Acts was written not primarily to give us a history of the primitive Church, but to furnish us with pattern insights into the nuts and bolts of what the Church not only was, but was meant to be. The New Testament was the ''Manufacturer's Handbook'' (to use a Harold Hill phrase), designed to show us the guts of the operation, not so much for our enlightenment historically as for our emulation existentially. After all, if the whole Old Testament is written for our instruction, then does it not follow that the New Testament will that much more present us with a working model?

My second proposition follows from the first: *As the epistles are normative for teaching, so the book of Acts is normative for life and experience of the Church.* God wants the present Church, the twentieth-century Church, to experience the same life and power the early Church experienced. God never intended the Church to seek authority structures outside those of the New Testament and thus the book of Acts becomes a crucial ''now'' book for the Church.

J.B. Phillips shares this enthusiasm. He writes, ''Here we are seeing the Church in its first youth, valiant and unspoiled—a body of ordinary men and women joined in an unconquerable fellowship never before seen on this earth. Yet we cannot help feeling disturbed as well as

moved, for *this surely is the Church as it was meant to be*"
(J.B. Phillips, *A Translation of the Acts of the Apostles*, p.
1, italics mine).

Part of my faith in the contemporaneity of the book of
Acts has to do with my confidence in Jesus as a leader. As
every great leader knows, he cannot expect his followers to
operate on the same level of genius when he is gone as
when he is present. Walter Lippman has well stated, "The
final test of the leader is that he leaves behind in other men
the conviction and the will to carry on. The genius of a
good leader is to leave behind him a situation which
common sense, without the grace of genius, can deal with
successfully." If the book of Acts is normative for the life
and experience of the Church, then Acts confronts us with
the necessity of decision: Will we go on to seek for real
New Testament power?

No one can accuse the twelve disciples of being a band
of geniuses. It is clear that Jesus simply left behind Him a
group of honest, hard-working, ordinary men to carry on
His work. A question confronts us: Where in the New
Testament do we see the actual life of the Church emerge
without Jesus there physically? Of course the answer is
obvious; in the book of Acts. If we want to see the new
creation fresh from the Creator's hands, glistening with the
touch of the Spirit, we have to view the book of Acts in a
new way.

Here I depart from traditional Protestant theology,
which has largely considered the book of Acts as necessary
for the launching of the Church, but hardly normative for
the present life and experience of the Church. The book of
Acts has been historically viewed as a book of evangelism

and church growth attended by extraordinary signs and miracles for the precise purpose of giving the Church its needed shove forward. As this purpose was accomplished, miracles dwindled and eventually almost disappeared. Acts, then, for traditional theology, is largely a book of antiquarian interest.

For those who have experienced the reality of Pentecost renewal, God has flung this book down from its snug place on the antiquarian shelf and now confronts us with a faith-decision of what He still purposes to do in His Church today. Acts demands a faith-response; it is a searching and demanding confirmation by the living Lord, from whom we cannot hide, and before whom all things lie naked and open; it is a challenge to become what we once were and what He wills that we should become again. Once the exciting miracles of the early Church have become living realities in our place and time, we are compelled to reevaluate our theology—not simply to become more experience-centered, and certainly those only committed to propositions about God have needed more experience of God—but to become more biblically true.

My second proposition, that *as the epistles are normative for the doctrine of the Church, so the principles of the book of Acts are normative for the life and experience of the Church,* may sound simple enough for those of us who have experienced the working of the charismata in our lives, but it is highly improbable that any theologian would have made that statement before 1950. ''The man with an experience is never at the mercy of a man with an argument.''

In other words, God in His mercy has visited our day

with the blessings of the Holy Spirit that have not been present in the Church to this degree and extent since the second century. Almost 1,800 years have passed without this sort of universal divine visitation. Quite possibly there always were pockets of charismatic experience within the Church, and I lean to the view that there were, but certainly nothing on the scale of what is now taking place. We can only stand in humility and thank the Lord.

If my thesis is correct, then, that Jesus left behind Him a Church which expressed His life (Acts) as well as His teaching (epistles), then this changes the theological approach to Acts enormously, because it calls for more than an antiquarian interest; it means the book of Acts becomes important to us today as a handbook of normative Christian experience. What occurred then can occur now. As Rufus Moseley said, "What Jesus was, He is; what He said, He says and what He did, He does." Theologically, the implications of that conclusion are mind-boggling.

Some will object that we cannot find this kind of pattern in the book of Acts at all. After all, which church in Acts would we adopt as the model? Certainly it could not be the Jerusalem church with its encrusted cultural and Jewish religious baggage, its practice of combining law and grace; nor could it be the Antioch church which stands more or less isolated in history. Would it then be Paul's churches founded in Asia Minor on a doctrine of pure grace or the Petrine churches with their strong Pauline flavor? In other words, what normative principles would distinguish all these churches?

I believe there are five: authority, community, sign gifts, worship, and bold witness.

These five characteristics appear to be normative for all the churches of Acts. Whether they are Petrine, Pauline, or Johannine churches, these five characteristics appear to be present.

First: *Authority*. The authority of the apostles was awesome. The Scripture speaks of how the people dedicated themselves to the apostolic doctrine. The necessity for spiritual authority cannot be overstressed. A New Testament Church simply cannot exist without a proper understanding and application of spiritual authority. If spiritual authority is rejected, there is no New Testament Church. For mid-twentieth-century America this must be a strange-sounding statement indeed. The American church, much more at home in the book of Judges where everyone "did what was right in his own eyes," than in Acts, finds it difficult to believe that a New Testament Church cannot exist without spiritual authority. But it is true. The proud, rebellious American heart has to bow to the incontrovertible evidence of Scripture: no spiritual authority, no Church. In fact, it really requires a revelation from God to understand the necessity for spiritual authority. Not instruction alone, but revelation. Beset on every side by strong-willed ministers and laymen alike who do their own thing, their own way, in their own time, blessing all their projects with the words, "The Lord told me," it seems virtually impossible to get people to even see the problem, let alone look for a solution. The typical reaction appears to be, "The Lord told him to do it so let him alone," no matter what dubious enterprise the man gets involved in. Today there is little spiritual accountability and hence decreasing credibility in the eyes of the Christian world. The "do your own thing" craze seems to have swept the charismatic movement into a rebellious individualism that appears to challenge the right of any man or authority to call for accountability in the matters of God. Yet biblically it is risky business for a man to declare, "The Lord told me," when in fact the Lord has not spoken.

The only act of defiance in the Church against the apostles recorded in Acts was the rebellion of Ananias and Sapphira who paid dearly for their rebellion against the Holy Spirit. Peter took great pains to explain to them the apostles were not standing on their own authority, but in the authority of the Holy Spirit, and the consequences of lying to that authority became visibly apparent to the whole Church. Some may react to this story as an Old Testament intrusion of the wrath of God, but it may in fact be the second most important miracle in the book of Acts, superseded only by the coming of the Spirit, because its consequences were so salutary in promoting and maintaining the purity and power of that Church.

It is quite apparent that the authority of the apostles is the glue that held the Church together. The power that emanated from them was so great that at various times people took them for more than men. The Philippian jailer fell on his knees, asking what he could do to be saved (Acts 16:25-30). On another occasion Paul and Barnabas were worshiped as Jupiter and Mercury (Acts 14:12-13), and in the last chapter of Acts the citizens of Malta first judged Paul to be a murderer, then called him a god (Acts 28:6).

Apostolic preaching was also remarkably authoritative.

It was the authority of Jesus himself reincarnated in them all over again—that same terrifying conviction, that almost arrogant humility persuading multitudes that they, the apostles, and they alone were bearers of the truth. Whether it was to Jews they preached, where they stressed the broken law, the need for justification and cleansing, or to Gentiles, where they persuaded by their miracles and powers that Christ had indeed destroyed the power of Satan, Jesus was presented as the answer.

Second: *Community (Koinonia).* A remarkable sense of community developed almost immediately in the early Church. It probably began with the ten days of prayer and fasting anticipating Pentecost. One is struck by the phrase, "with one accord," that occurs so many times in the opening chapters of Acts. There was a sense of unity unlike anything since the Garden of Eden. The "one accordness" appears to be the unifying factor for the whole community. Today we seize on their sharing of material possessions as a remarkable characteristic, but really the wonder work of the early Church was its unity. It was considered so binding and strong that it transcended family, race, and culture. Christians belonged, as it were, to a universal higher family. Those who had more, shared as a matter of course with those who had little or nothing.

The principle of equality didn't mean that all had the same amount, but it did mean that those who had an excess shared with those who had nothing. It was obvious to the early apostles that the families, houses, fathers, mothers, brothers, and sisters Jesus had promised in such abundance, in fact, one hundredfold to His followers, had indeed come to pass literally—in the Church, the body of Christ. No wonder no convert strayed far from such a close-knit family.

This remarkable community spirit made the whole Church truly one so that Gentiles gave very generously, and almost excessively, to poor Jewish believers in Jerusalem. *That* has to be a first in recorded history!

The community had a remarkably competent lay leadership as well. While the apostles remained in Jerusalem (Acts 8:1, 4), the laymen scattered throughout the region and began dozens of small churches wherever they went. Even the men chosen to serve the people as deacons (Acts 6) were men filled with the Spirit who were also tremendous witnesses. The first martyr, Stephen, came from among them.

The people caught on to this life style in an incredible way. According to Acts, Paul only spent three short weeks in Thessalonica and yet had no scruples about leaving that baby church on its own. They were so remarkably alive and vital that they not only came to maturity, but reached out to the adjoining provinces of Achaia and Macedonia with the gospel. Paul commended them for their outspoken witness (1 Thess. 1:8).

Government in the community was minimal but adequate. Elders or overseers (including pastors, teachers, shepherds, bishops, presbyters) and deacons were the mainstay of the local church. There is some evidence of local prophets (1 Cor. 14:29-33). Universal prophets (like Agabus) and evangelists appeared to have had more of a traveling ministry. The churches operated on a local level almost autonomously as long as everything went well, but when trouble arose, as in the case of the Judaizers in Galatia, and the local elders lacked the knowledge or authority to correct the doctrinal problem, the apostle always asserted his authority effectively. Hodge says, "Apostolic authority was infallible." That may be going too far, but formidable enough it was.

There was, of course, no such thing as denominations, for the only recognized division was on the basis of locality. As the World Council of Churches put it in a 1963 manifesto, "The church is simply all the people of God gathered together in one place."

In Ephesians 2, Paul gives theological articulation to this principle by saying that God took two peoples, some near at hand and some far away, and made of them one new man, thus establishing peace by the blood of the cross. The new man is a new creation, the new body in Christ.

Third: *Sign-gifts.* The sign-gifts were as numerous or more numerous than they were in Jesus' day. At times, the very shadow of the apostles healed (Acts 5:15). Blessed handkerchiefs brought relief, and exorcisms as remarkable as any in the life of Jesus occurred at the hands of the apostles. Even resurrections from the dead occurred (Acts 9:36-41). The theology of the sign-gifts is made clear throughout Acts but particularly in Acts 4 when the church in trouble is praying for help. As they clearly state, they will preach as God heals. Sign-gifts, in other words, were to be the external evidences of the veracity of the apostolic witness. Authentic miracles have that power even among the most sophisticated scoffers. As one of my students reported one day on a discussion he held with his philosophy professor, "If an authentic miracle were done here in this room, what would you say?"

The professor admitted, "I would have to change my philosophy of life."

Sign-gifts were indispensable for the proclamation of the gospel. All the evidence shows that every evangelist in the New Testament practiced them. Without them they would not have been able to get to first base among the hardened sinners and scoffers of that day. No one could doubt but that they were to be the accrediting signs to the heathen that God was among them.

One cannot but speculate on how much faster the gospel would have spread throughout the world during the great nineteenth-century missionary outreach if miracles had always attended preaching. Even today, the pentecostal groups who practice the sign-gifts are showing astronomical growth in the number of members and adherents they gain to their cause; particularly in Africa, Asia, and South America. The sign-gifts still demonstrate in an irrefutable way the power of the living God.

Most theologians have viewed the sign-gifts as interesting and even necessary signs for the launching of the Church, but only of historical interest to us today. That was far from the mind-set of the early Church. I remember once asking F.F. Bruce, an expert on Acts, "Dr. Bruce, in writing Acts did Luke understand that the sign-gifts were to cease at the end of the apostolic age?"

He responded, "No, Luke undoubtedly felt they would go on indefinitely. The apostles did not conceive that miracles would cease." Since Luke felt this way, and he was at pains to give a good historical account, why should we not also look for the sign-gifts? There is every reason to believe that the atmosphere of the early Church was in complete consistency with Mark 16:8, whether or not this is part of the original text: "And these signs shall follow them that believe." No adequate theological reason for the cessation of miracles has ever been developed from the pages of the New Testament.

Fourth: *Worship.* The worship experience of the early Church has almost become legendary. It was reverential and majestic. We know this because they enjoyed the full favor of the Jewish community, known for its awe of God. But it was also joyous and jubilant, because the risen Lord was still among them. Their worship was such a precious experience that not a day passed but they gathered to celebrate the joy of the Lord. The accounts in Acts show us a community of people who simply could not stay away from each other. They were always breaking bread together, and probably sharing Communion on a daily basis. They ate together with "glad and sincere hearts." Again the worship was characterized by heavy lay participation. Everyone brought his gift to the church. First Corinthians 14:26 shows us how it worked. There were songs in the Spirit, there were prophecies, there were teachings, there were revelations, and no one who genuinely had something from the Lord was excluded. Their corporate worship was the main source of their joy and power in evangelism. Striking parallels could be found in Africa today. Some years ago, Bud Sickler told me that the phenomenal growth of a native pentecostal group from several hundred to over 100,000 in thirteen years was due to two things: worship and witness.

Fifth: *Confrontational witnessing.* It is impossible to read the book of Acts without being challenged and perhaps appalled at the audacity of the apostles. They had a terrifying boldness that struck consternation to their sophisticated and intelligent Jewish adversaries. They took on the religious establishment in such a bold way that it almost takes our breath away. They demonstrated their right to speak by their healing powers, and an astonishing multitude followed them, convinced of their authenticity. This bold witness was so contagious that hardly were new Christians born into the kingdom, than they were out sharing their faith with any and all who would listen.

These five normative characteristics of the Church in Acts were never meant to be simply delightful historical reminders of what the primitive Church once was, but pattern-witnesses to the glorious future of the eschatological community—what she was meant to be, and what by God's grace she shall become as we once again allow the Holy Spirit freedom in the life and fabric of our future together as the body of Christ.

What a tremendous day to be alive! All over the world, wherever there has been a touch of the Spirit, there is a search for New Testament reality; among all Christian traditions the Bible has become increasingly central to faith and practice. David du Plessis assures us that the Roman Catholic church today is distributing more Bibles than Protestants and Pentecostals put together. Present-day ecumenical councils aver that their expressed objective is to "go back all the way to Jerusalem." Even where imbalance of all kinds exists—and certainly excesses in discipleship, "faith teaching," exorcism, exclusivism and reductionistic thinking do exist—even then that imbalance is a witness to the fertility and amazing virility of a lively faith. God is alive and well. Our problems are stepping stones to the triumph of Christ.

The Church has a tremendous future. Peter Wagner estimates that more people will be won to Christ in the next twenty-five years than in any comparable time in Church history. Even at the present rate of increase in Africa, it is estimated that there will be 350,000,000 believers by the year 2000.

As we approach the end of the age, we can only give thanks to God that in His infinite mercy He has brought us by His Spirit to a new frontier, a frontier as exciting and dynamic as the first frontier at Pentecost; as fraught with peril and risk as when the Church first emerged, but with a promise as bright as springtime. The Church is on the march. We have a chance to be the "glorious Church." Let us not miss it.

Appendix

A Methodology for Ecumenical Theology

For the emerging "church of the restoration" there are some sticky problems and differences which demand answers. Who is to say who is right? Is there some kind of universal standard which can be accepted by all? More important, what are the boundary lines for Christian fellowship? Whom may we call brothers? From whom do we dissociate? On what grounds?

Since the fifth century, Christians in general have agreed, at least in theory, with the Augustinian dictum, "In the essentials, unity; in non-essentials, liberty; but in all things, charity." In actual practice, this guideline has been conspicuous by its absence. Not only is that true but it is one of the indisputable facts of history that we tend to fight hardest those who are nearest to us in doctrine. Baptists don't fight the Eastern Orthodox; they fight fellow Baptists. Nazarenes and Pentecostals find the same cultural and theological parentage; yet the infighting among them, particularly over the issue of speaking in tongues, has turned into a mutual exclusion and doctrinal rigidity one usually reserves for his foes. What, then, should our approach be to those with whom we disagree in the charismatic movement? What should our attitude be to those who have also borne the brunt of persecution and misunderstanding because of their experience in the Holy Spirit, those who have also paid the price in loss of friends and denominational ties? If a choice has to be made between an overzealous faith or the patent disbelief in miracles that characterizes much of present-day evangelicalism, then let us opt for the "faith teaching." Shall we term those with whom we disagree "heretic," or refuse them the right hand of Christian fellowship? Should we not rather embrace them as brothers and thank God for the thousands who can testify to changed lives and lifted faith because of their teaching? If there are to be disagreements, let them devolve about principle, not personalities; let disagreements concern issues, not people. If there are corrections to be made, let them be made in the spirit of Christian love and concern. This is not to abdicate our responsibility to speak the truth; it is simply to make sure that it is done in love (Eph. 4:15).

A far more serious problem exists for many Protestant charismatics in finding a common basis for fellowship with the widely varying doctrinal positions of Roman Catholicism and Eastern Orthodoxy. When one approaches the fellowship problem theologically, the differences seem almost insurmountable. For starters, what right-thinking Protestant could accept papal infallibility, the Assumption of Mary, the doctrine of indulgences, purgatory, the treasury of merit or prayer through the saints? How could Protestants be happy with Orthodox theology that approaches God in His essence by a theology of denial? How can he view the layman as essentially a spectator? How can he fellowship with a group which does virtually no evangelistic preaching to its own constituency?

Or, to turn the table, what dedicated Roman Catholic could ever be comfortable with the Protestant theology which looks upon the Holy Communion as purely symbolic, which views baptism as an ordinance rather than a sacrament, which has such a low view of the Church that it does not literally view it as the body of Christ on earth, which vests spiritual authority in the congregation rather than the apostolic order?

Yet the Spirit not only commands us to fellowship with these "different" believers, He has himself opened the way and been the causative agent in some of the most beautifully moving experiences twentieth-century Christendom has witnessed. For us, the miracle of Pentecost may not be so much speaking in tongues as in loving our Catholic and Orthodox brothers. Historians will undoubtedly view the charismatic movement as the most powerful force in present-day ecumenism; but they will be hard pressed to find a historical explanation apart from the supernatural power of the Spirit himself, since nothing but the Spirit's overwhelming us has made possible what is now happening universally in Christendom. If the great miracle of the first Pentecost was an evangelistic explosion, the great miracle of the second Pentecost is a Christian unity at the grass roots. What man could not do, the Holy Spirit has done. Here we are, with a growing spiritual unity in the midst of irreconcilable doctrinal differences. How do we maintain our dearly held distinctives while encouraging unity? Is there a way out of the dilemma?

For hundreds of years the Western Church has approached Christianity propositionally. That is, the terms of Christianity have always been stated in such a way that agreement with certain propositions spelled orthodoxy, disagreement, heresy. There is a need for precision in theology; but, unfortunately, it can also lead to some serious and unnecessary breaches in fellowship through a misunderstanding of what is really being said. The question is, are we right in judging others worthy of fellowship purely on the basis of doctrine?

For example, for hundreds of years the Armenian church has been considered heretical because it held to the doctrine of the Monophysites. The Monophysites believed that the divine nature in Jesus transformed His human nature so that the whole became divine, even though some human characteristics remained. Clearly the doctrine, if defined in those terms, is heretical. However, while I was on sabbatical in Israel, Monsigneur Mancini of Jerusalem informed me that the Armenians were not heretical and that their doctrine of Christ was perfectly orthodox. He gave me to understand that the whole misunderstanding has been a matter of semantics. A schism of hundreds of years occurred through an avoidable error. Mancini assured me that today the Armenian church is considered orthodox by the Roman Catholic hierarchy.

Experience has a way of mellowing our understanding. For years I held with Barth that the doctrine of the physical

Resurrection of Jesus Christ is the *sine qua non* of Christianity. It is the watershed that divided the sheep from the goats. I reasoned, how can a man be a Christian who does not believe in the Resurrection? Doesn't Paul make Christ's Resurrection the central dogma, and doesn't he argue that the whole structure collapses without this central Christian understanding (1 Cor. 15:12-19)? Since Paul puts all of his eggs in one basket, why can't we follow suit? Those who believe in the Resurrection are on the side of the angels; those who do not, simply are not in.

Doctrinally this is safe ground. The New Testament makes it clear that the physical Resurrection of Jesus Christ from the dead is the foundation of all New Testament teaching.

But the disturbing question arises, is it possible to be intellectually sub-Christian, even non-Christian, and still be saved? Is it possible through bad theology or just plain ignorance to believe that the body of Jesus still lies in Israel and yet be truly born again? Is it conceivable that a man could be thoroughly and soundly converted by calling on the Name of the Lord and not realize the importance of Jesus? These last two questions are existential realities for me in two experiences I find theologically inexplicable.

A few years ago I met a fine young Presbyterian minister who responded to the Spirit and received the experience of the Spirit's infilling with the evidence of speaking in tongues. One day he raised a question about the finality of the death of Jesus. Because of what he had been taught in seminary, he thought Jesus' bones were still decaying in Israel. Incredulous, I briefly explained the Resurrection of Jesus from the dead using the familiar Pauline arguments concerning the necessity of the physical Resurrection for true faith. He didn't say much. I left perplexed, wondering how his faith in Christ related to a dead Jesus.

Some time later I saw him.

"Say, Chuck," he said, "something strange happened to me after you explained the physical Resurrection of Jesus. Something inside began to sing and the Spirit told me, 'Chuck is right! Jesus really did rise physically from the dead.' I was so happy I hardly knew what to do! My whole life has new meaning. This is the first time I ever realized Jesus was raised from the dead! It has been a transforming experience."

Question: Was he born anew before he made the wonderful discovery of Christ's Resurrection? Although this experience has never been explained satisfactorily theologically, it seems to me Fred's heart was ahead of his head, and God honored his heart.

The second incident was equally disturbing theologically. Some years ago, a friend of mine was weary of the life he was living. He called on God to save him. Floods of loving forgiveness poured through him. His life changed dramatically. He began to read his Bible and pray. He attended church regularly. As far as he understood, his new relationship was solely between the Father and himself. Two years went by. Then he recognized Jesus as the agent of God's mercy. The disturbing thing about this incident is that to this day he insists his conversion occurred two years before he knew Christ had anything to do with it. Was he saved before he recognized that it was through Christ salvation came?

I am not attempting to downgrade the importance of

good theology or sound doctrine. It is the main task of my academic life. But I am raising a question. Is a "proper theology of the Word" sufficient grounds for including or excluding people from Christian fellowship? Is adherence to a set of propositions a sufficient test for *koinonia*? Is it possible that many who assent to the doctrines are not "in," and that many who cannot assent to some of the basic doctrines are not "out"? Will God surprise us with those we thought were "in" who are "out," and with those we thought were "out" who are "in"?

From Luther onwards, evangelical theology has leaned heavily on assent to certain doctrines as decisive for Christian fellowship. I believe this approach alone is inadequate and neglects the central thrust of the book of Acts, the dynamism of the Spirit. Classical Protestantism has neglected a proper theology of the Spirit and in so doing has destroyed the bipolar balance between the Word and the Spirit which the reformers so desperately tried to preserve. This has resulted in an imbalance in theology that still cries out for rectification. The greatest need in theology today is an adequate theology of the Spirit. We need a theology that is comprehensive enough to embrace the theology of Paul while including the historical interests of Luke, a theology that is equally faithful to Acts and the epistles.

Since the Christian Church precedes the existence of systematic theology, it is clear that theology must be a function of the Church. From its earliest days, the Christian community has always been a teaching body and it is out of obedience to the Lord of the Church that theology must arise. It is not that there is a science of

Church dogmatics that gives rise to teaching in the Church. It is rather that the Church, as a teaching community, produces theology.

Thus it is not because there is a science of Christian dogmatics that we have Christian teaching, but, conversely, Christian teaching is the cause of dogmatics. (Emil Brunner, *Dogmatics*, Vol. 1, p. 4.)

After all, it was two hundred years after the death of Christ before the first systematic theology arose.

Objections

1. The necessity for serious theology at all is questioned today in charismatic circles. On many fronts, there is a dismaying salute to anti-intellectualism. Instead, a kind of pop theology is making the rounds with different formulas guaranteeing success. At the present time, charismatic theology, at least on the lay level, is reductionist. Everything can be reduced to a formula that supplies success, health and wealth, where you can write your own ticket with God. Splashed with liberal doses of crypto-Christian Scientism on the one hand, or veering dangerously close to spiritual magic on the other, a charismatic theology purified by expressing the whole counsel of God desperately needs to be written.

2. A second objection to theology arises from within

the Christian community itself. The Bible calls us to action. It is, after all, obedience and fellowship that counts, not theological theory. It is encounter with the living Christ that is real, that is necessary, not the narrow confines of an impersonal doctrinal authority inserted between us and and living Lord himself. "Doctrine divides; the Spirit unites." However, without the surveyor's charts and compasses, the Church can fellowship itself right off the theological map. The Church cannot survive without theology, whether it is systematized or not.

3. A third objection is historical. It can be pointed out that for 1500 years Israel existed as a religious community with no systematic theology. The Bible itself knows nothing of systematic theology. The early Christian Church at the time of its greatest purity and power produced no dogmatics. So why is theology important?

It's true Israel had no systematic theology but her alternative proved to be legalism, operation by precedent. That is a dead-end street. And although it is also true that the early Church had no systematic theology, she had a wealth of apostolic teaching. Inevitably, as heresies erupted within and intellectual challenges arose without, apostolic teaching led to theological reflection and theological reflection led to systematic theology.

Theology as an Act of Faith

First, we must concede that theology is not of the essence of the Church. The Church could and did exist without anything like systematic theology for many years. Theology is not, therefore, an absolute necessity. But is it not a relative necessity? Brunner finds its relative necessity in a threefold historical source, the war against false doctrine, the teachings arising early in the Church, and in biblical exegesis (Brunner, Vol. 1, p. 10). The New Testament is not really a book of theology, but from the records we have in the Bible, it is possible to construct a "theology of the apostles" honoring their differences while marveling at the underlying unity of the apostolic account. Anyone who claims he teaches simply "what the Bible teaches" is theologically naive. Witness the Southern Baptists who claim the whole canon of Scripture as their only guide for doctrine, yet spiritualize away the miracles. Others use a complex device known as dispensational theology to explain away the dynamic expressed in 1 Corinthians 12 and 14.

For any group to claim it follows the Bible and the Bible alone is historically and psychologically naive. Conscious and unconscious selectivity goes into any process of teaching; teaching involves systematizing thoughts, and systematizing thoughts about doctrine eventually creates a systematic theology. If Paul, for example, had been born in Augustine's century he very likely would have fathered a very good systematic theology. Furthermore, the task of theology is never completed; it never exists as a given for the next generation to receive without further theological reflection. He who is Truth must continually be sought anew in the many truths witnessed to by the apostles, and the "faith once delivered" needs continual theological reflection in the service of the Church.

Theology must be understood as an act of faith. It calls for strenuous intellectual effort with all the faculties of attention and concentration, understanding and judgment that are necessary in all human enterprises. But it also calls for an act of faith that lays hold of Him who leads us into all truth (John 16:13). Only in faith can the theologian properly perform his task. Only by faith can he address the truth about the Truth. "Thus dogmatics is only possible as an act of faith, in the determination of human action by listening, and as obedience towards Jesus Christ" (Barth, *Dogmatics*, Vol. 1, Part 1, p. 18). Thus the task of theology must be understood in the role of a servant; it functions best as servant of the Church. Barth found that the theologians had no help for the preacher because their theology had become university-centered rather than church-centered. He was shocked when his professors of theology moved easily into the philosophy department. He was even more shocked to find them in agreement with some of the war aims of the Nazis. He correctly determined that their ethical malfunction was due to an inadequate theology, and upon examination he found the whole movement of theology from Schleiermacher's day onward to be the wrong direction, from man to God rather than from God to man. He decried theologians who perceived their task as dishing out contemporary ideas in a slightly different form as theology.

Theologians have no mandate from God to write merely for one another; to do so is not only an act of disobedience to God, it is an act of intellectual pride which is disservice to the Church. As Dr. Howard Ervin, my colleague at ORU, has said, "Theology is the queen of the sciences but the handmaiden of the body of Christ."

Yes, theology must be viewed as an act of faith. A bad Christian can never make a good theologian. The theologian must rely upon the Holy Spirit to lead him into all truth, and all he writes may only be viewed as a moving point and not a final destination. His work must be reexamined in the next generation for the possibility of greater fidelity to the Word of God. This is the task of theology.

Can There Be a Theological Methodology for Handling New Doctrine in Charismatic Circles?

Without question, the charismatic movement is the most ecumenical movement in the world today. Surprisingly, it has swept across existing denominational boundaries with the force of a hurricane and has created an atmosphere of trust and joy among Christians not present since the days of the apostles. It has brought the three great traditions of Christianity together in a unity of the Spirit that defies human explanation and at the practical level it has achieved a level of mutual commitment that exceeds the best efforts of ecumenically minded theologians in all preceding centuries.

But its very success brings some attendant problems. What do we do when a new teaching or doctrine emerges that threatens the unity of the Church? How do we handle new revelations not specifically taught in Scripture? What happens when an individual or a group of individuals develop teachings that subvert existing loyalties, allegiances, and church affiliations? Is there some theological methodology we can follow that will be mutually agreeable to prevent discord and strife? To what objective authority can we appeal?

I have limited myself to a discussion of new teaching, new doctrine, because at this point in history, there is very little any of us can do to change the magisteriums of our three great traditions. Ecumenical councils, doctrinal standards and church traditions all vary so greatly that any attempt to reopen discussion of past doctrinal differences, at least at this stage, must be treated with great caution. Unless carefully handled, it could prove disruptive to the swelling unity of the Spirit and divert us from His calling to healing in the Body.

Admittedly, authority is the Achilles heel of revealed religion. How can we "prove" our authority? What proofs are adequate to float the "givenness" of authority? How does one demonstrate his authority as over and against other authorities?

These are real questions, but they need not overly concern us, since ours is a common faith in which the Scriptures are, for all three traditions, in some sense authoritative. Although these traditions vary about the place of the Bible in their understanding of the total content of authority, yet all agree that Scripture expresses the "spokenness" of God.

Let me then suggest that one part of our methodology will be a theology of the Word determined by contextual scientific exegesis. This involves an empathetic response to the biblical thought form. As much as possible, it means crawling inside the epidermis of the apostle who wrote and hearing in faith what those who first listened heard. It means extracting the meaning of the disputed passage in its whole context, then testing that meaning in other parallel passages and finally drawing out conclusions in terms of the whole teaching of Scripture.

My early training taught me that the first question to be asked was, "What does the Bible say to us?" I think that is not the proper first question. The first question is, "What did the Scripture mean to those who wrote it and to those who first heard it?" Contextual scientific exegesis is the only way I know to answer that question. Even then our knowledge is partial, fragmentary and incomplete. The first question, then, is not, "What does the passage say to me," but, "What did it mean to the man who wrote it and to the men who first heard it?" This attitude is the:

. . . mind set of the prophets and the apostles. It is not the attitude of observers . . . nor of philosophers, but that of witnesses, of people who, whatever else they may be, speak as those who are grounded in the reality of the 'and God spoke' as an absolute presupposition. (Karl Barth, *Christliche Dogmatik*, p. 403, quoted in Müeller, *Karl Barth*, p. 36)

Proper exegesis means that we move from faith to faith. It does not mean we will ever free ourselves completely from the philosophical remnants of our particular heritage, nor does it mean we will fully escape our own experience and history, but it does mean that the controlling factor in all our theological thinking will be the Word of God. "If the Word dominates, the philosophical and other elements utilized by the theologian will be subordinated to their rightful center'' (*Ibid.*, p. 36). Faith, by its very nature, drives us to a better understanding. Thus we can subscribe to the Anselmic dictum, *fides quaerens intellectum* (faith in search of understanding), as a proper theological methodology. As new teachings arise, they can be tested by scientific exegesis in the present life of the Church.

Four Categories of New Teaching to Be Reviewed

These teachings will probably fall into one of four categories. They may be thoroughly biblical doctrines hitherto neglected by the Church, or old doctrines being renewed and brought to our attention again by the Holy Spirit's present activity, or they may be teachings not explicitly found in the Scriptures, but generally judged not to be of such a nature as to disturb the unity of the Church. Such doctrines might include Church forms and polity where considerable latitude is permissible. These are doctrinal *adiaphora* (indifferent teachings). Finally, they may be teachings judged to be injurious to the life of the Church because they are contrary to the plain sense of Scripture or to the sense of the Spirit in the Church. Both principles are important. Where doctrines, for example, such as ultimate reconciliation, are taught (i.e., that even the devil will eventually be saved), grave consequences for contextual scientific exegesis result. However, not only would palpably false doctrine be rejected, but also teachings and movements which threaten the unity of the movement by creating division and schism in the Spirit-filled community. It is conceivable that a right doctrine could be premature and prove disruptive to the unity of the Church.

A good method of exegesis should be the controlling factor in biblical interpretation. This does not mean we look for a mechanical precision in every detail of Scripture or that we opt for a word for-word literalism or even that a proper exegesis of the verses mmediately preceding or following the teaching in question invariably establishes the truth. But it does mean that the Scriptures hold for all three Christian traditions the conviction that God has spoken in an intelligible fashion and that what He has said is authoritative for men in matters of faith and practice. A good example of where the immediate context cannot solve the problem of meaning is found in Ecclesiastes 3:18 and 19. This cannot be considered normative biblical teaching.

I said to myself concerning the sons of men, God has surely tested them in order for them to see that they are but beasts. For the fate of the sons of men and the fate of the beasts is the same. As one dies, so does the other; indeed they all have the same breath and there is no advantage for man over beast, for all is vanity.

These verses in essence teach a sub-biblical understanding of the nature of man. Here the hermeneutical problem is best resolved by an appeal to the analogy of faith which interprets Scripture in the light of other Scripture. The fundamental question to be answered is what was the principle, the intent, the purpose generated in the author's mind and what properly establishes the boundaries between what can be and what cannot be inferred from what he said.

The word "scientific" means that the methodology of science is also applicable to Scripture. Science proceeds by proposing a theory and then testing that theory by the actual findings of the concrete, controlled experiment. In this way, a self-corrective principle is built into the search for truth. In the same way an exegete may have some idea of the meaning of the text, but his work of exegesis constantly corrects and supplements his prior understanding so that a fuller and more adequate theology may emerge. Calvin furnishes a good example. When he first completed the *Institutes of the Christian Religion* at age twenty-six, it was a slim volume. As he progressed with his exegesis of the rest of the Scriptures, the volume grew in size until it became the formidable piece of Reformation theology we now have.

Christ himself, however, is the final interpreter of Scripture. Christ is sovereign Lord of all Scripture, just as he is sovereign Lord of the Church, and all teachings must, therefore, finally be interpreted Christologically. That is the final step in a "theology of the Word."

Four Steps to a Theological Methodology

Practically speaking, this course of action calls for a four-step operation. Let us say we are interested in the biblical doctrine of the word "flesh." We might begin by exegeting Paul's use of the word "flesh." But that is not enough. There is more to do. The study begins all over again summarizing what other biblical authors have to say about "flesh." Still the task is not completed. The exegete must then grasp what is taught in the Bible as a whole. It is at this point that the task of the systematic theologian begins. He must take the results of the biblical study and interpret it in terms of what can be understood from his own setting and century. This is *fides quaerens intellectum*, faith in search of understanding.

Of course, such studies are provisional and each generation will have to wrestle anew with exegetical problems and further refinements of theological reflection. As the old Puritan said, "God hath yet more light to shed from His Word." This explains why theology must always remain a moving point and why sound doctrine always proves to be a task "which is never ended. . . . The one truth of Christ is refracted in the manifold doctrines of the apostles; but it is the task of the church—which has to proclaim the truth of Christ; and thus also has to teach—to seek continually for the one light of truth within these refractions" (Brunner, Vol. 1, p. 13).

A Theology of Revelation

In American political life, there comes a time in Congress when no vote is necessary. A certain feeling pervades the atmosphere and that spirit or feeling is designated a "sense of the Senate." There is also a "sense of the Spirit." This second ingredient in a charismatic theological methodology may be called a theology of revelation. The dynamism of the Spirit cannot be contained in old wineskins. It is not enough to do sound exegesis; there must also be an experiential "awareness" in theology which relies directly on the Holy Spirit for its sense of direction. This might be labeled a "theology of experience." Of all movements in the world today, surely the charismatic movement must make room for experiential theology. This theology of revelation focuses on the "nowness" of the crisis, inquiring as to what the "Spirit says to the churches."

In classical Protestantism, theology has had two basic approaches; one emphasizes God's divine action; the other focuses on man's experience of and response to God (Robert K. Johnston, "Of Tidy Doctrine and Truncated Experience," *Christianity Today,* Feb. 18, 1977, p. 10). The former is represented by Calvin and his "theology of the Word." The latter is represented by men such as Wesley and Schleiermacher, who stress a theology of experience. Which approach is correct?

It seems to me that the Bible makes room for both. If one emphasizes a theology of the Word to the exclusion of experience, he runs the risk of traditional evangelical theology which is justly criticized as being largely irrelevant. If he stresses solely a theology of experience, he runs the counter risk of the quagmires of subjectivity. Schleiermacher did not escape these quicksands.

Robert K. Johnston states: "If Word and Spirit can be held in dynamic union, then experiential theology has the possibility of becoming definitive for the life and witness of the evangelical church today. If not, such a theology must be called to task and dismissed as sub-biblical, as Schleiermacher's was. The Word cannot take the place of the Spirit, as has often happened in conservative circles. But neither can the Word be ignored" (*Ibid.,* p. 12).

Must Open into the Word

A theology of the Spirit must open into the Word. It can neither contradict nor subvert the Word but it enriches the Word through experience. For example, only when an awareness of the Spirit comes can men distinguish between two kinds of tongues (1 Cor. 14:18-19). What can this passage mean? He speaks in tongues more than anybody else and at the same time he doesn't care to speak in tongues in the church. No wonder exegetes from ancient times down to the present day have been puzzled!

But for us who have experienced this particular *charismata*, it is perfectly clear. Paul is distinguishing between devotional tongues and tongues in the church meeting. For example, I pray daily in the language of the Spirit but over the past fifteen years I have only been used twice in giving a message in tongues. Here it is clear that my experience of the Spirit has illuminated my "theology of the Word."

Must Follow Biblical Precedent

The Council at Jerusalem is most instructive in this movement from the crisis moment in the experience of the early Church to a loving solution by recourse to an immediate experience of the Spirit as Teacher. At Jerusalem, a totally Jewish church, the believing Pharisees mounted a frontal challenge to the Pauline doctrine of justification by faith. Any believer, Gentile or not, had to be circumcised. They had a "theology of the Word" to prove it. If the only source of authority had been the written Word, the Old Testament, propositional revelation interpreted by rabbinical legalism, the believing Pharisees would have won their case hands down. No doubt about it.

Moses made no provision for men to become members of the household of faith without first becoming Jews. The Gentiles could not have been received into the *ecclesia* without a full proselyte ceremony. How was the situation to be handled? Peter argued from experience; experience obviously led and directed by the Spirit, but experience nonetheless.

He recalled for them his unforgettable experience at Caesarea where the Holy Spirit had sovereignly fallen on the household of Cornelius without circumcision and without baptism. In essence, he asked these theologians of the Word, "How can you be more fussy than God? If God gave them the Holy Spirit without distinction, how can you make a distinction?" (Acts 15:6-11).

Fortunately, the council was alive to the Spirit. Pentecost had changed their *modus operandi*. They consulted the Holy Spirit directly and He did not disappoint them. Through James, the Spirit illuminated some ancient prophesies, which gave to the Church a new understanding which has become definitive for believers to this day. It is interesting to note that the Spirit did not proceed without the Word but through the Word. It was circulated in the famous Jerusalem letter: "For it has seemed good to the Holy Spirit and to us to lay upon you no greater burden than these necessary things: that you abstain from what has been sacrificed to idols and from blood and from what is strangled and from unchastity" (Acts 15:28-30a).

We must note that James's argument, under the guidance of the Spirit, moves from Peter's experience with Cornelius and his household to a new interpretation of some ancient prophesies. It was not the Spirit without the Word, but the Spirit speaking through the Word that made this council the second great milestone in the history of the early Church. A true theology of revelation always moves in harmony with the Word, although it often contradicts contemporary *interpretations* of the Word.

In our approach to a theological methodology for the charismatic movement, we need a dynamic union between the Spirit and the Word; a bipolar approach which combines a "theology of the Word" with a "theology of the Spirit."

In light of the fact that God has called us to the concrete task of working together to promote the unity of the brethren, I suggest that we agree to submit our major new understandings for counsel and guidance before going public. One possibility for handling such matters might be to appoint a committee on theological concerns and another committee which would seek the Lord for a "sense of the Spirit" among our varied constituencies.

Notes

[1]William F. Arndt and F. Wilbur Gingrich, *A Greek English Lexicon of the New Testament*, pp. 478-480; pp. 742, 3.
Theologians have debated the possibility of Jesus sinning for centuries. The classic Orthodox doctrine teaches that in His divine nature, Jesus was not able to sin; but in His human nature, He was able not to sin. If the real possibility of sin did not exist for Jesus, He could not have been tempted "in every respect . . . as we are, yet without sinning" (Hebrews 4:15).

[2]Robert Braman, "From the Greek World to the Gospel According to John." Unpublished paper, 1977.

[3]W.E. Vine, *Expository Dictionary of New Testament Words*, Revell, 1962, p. 230.

[4]Thayer, p. 382.

[5]Franz Delitzsch, *Biblical Commentary on the Prophesies of Isaiah*, Volume II, William B. Eerdman's Publishing Company, p. 316.

[6]*The Expositor's Greek New Testament*, Volume III, p. 110.

[7]John Calvin, *Commentary on the Epistles of Paul the Apostle to the Corinthians*, Eerdman's Publishing Company, p. 374.

[8]A.T. Robertson, *Word Pictures in the New Testament*, Broadman Press, p. 265. T.E.G.M.T., p. 111.

[9]Calvin, p. 374.

[10]*Ibid.*, pp. 373-374.

[11]C.K. Barrett, *A Commentary on the Second Epistle to the Corinthians*, Harper and Row, p. 315.

[12]James Strong, *The Exhaustive Concordance of the Bible*, Abingdon Press, New York and Nashville.
Greek Dictionary of the New Testament, p. 58.

[13]Charles Price, *The Real Faith*, Charles S. Price Publishing Company, Pasadena, CA, pp. 58-69.

[14]W.E. Vine, *New Testament Greek Grammar*, Zondervan Publishing House, p. 182.

[15]*Ibid.*

[16]William F. Arndt and F. Wilbur Gingrich, *A Greek-English Lexicon of the New Testament*, University of Chicago Press, p. 668.